Wireless Networks
first-step

Jim Geier

Cisco Press
800 East 96th Street
Indianapolis, IN 46240

Wireless Networks
first-step

Jim Geier

Copyright© 2005 Cisco Systems, Inc.

Cisco Press logo is a trademark of Cisco Systems, Inc.

Published by:
Cisco Press
800 East 96th Street
Indianapolis, IN 46240 USA

Printed in the United States of America 1 2 3 4 5 6 7 8 9 0

First Printing August 2004

Library of Congress Cataloging-in-Publication Number: 2003111981

ISBN: 1-58720-111-9

Warning and Disclaimer

Publisher
John Wait

Editor-in-Chief
John Kane

Cisco Representative
Anthony Wolfenden

**Cisco Press
Program Manager**
Nannette M. Noble

Executive Editor
Brett Bartow

Acquisitions Editor
Michelle Grandin

Production Manager
Patrick Kanouse

Development Editor
Andrew Cupp

Senior Project Editor
San Dee Phillips

Copy Editor
Laura Williams

Technical Editors
Joel Barrett
D. Ed Lamprecht
Joseph Roth

Editorial Assistant
Tammi Barnett

Book and Cover Designer
Louisa Adair

Compositor
Mark Shirar

Indexer
Brad Herriman

Proofreader
Tonya Cupp

Feedback Information

At Cisco Press, our goal is to create in-depth technical books of the highest quality and value. Each book is crafted with care and precision, undergoing rigorous development that involves the unique expertise of members from the professional technical community.

Readers' feedback is a natural continuation of this process. If you have any comments regarding how we could improve the quality of this book, or otherwise alter it to better suit your needs, you can contact us through email at feedback@ciscopress.com. Please make sure to include the book title and ISBN in your message.

We greatly appreciate your assistance.

Trademark Acknowledgments

All terms mentioned in this book that are known to be trademarks or service marks have been appropriately capitalized. Cisco Press or Cisco Systems, Inc. cannot attest to the accuracy of this information. Use of a term in this book should not be regarded as affecting the validity of any trademark or service mark.

Corporate and Government Sales

Cisco Press offers excellent discounts on this book when ordered in quantity for bulk purchases or special sales.

For more information please contact: **U.S. Corporate and Government Sales** 1-800-382-3419 corpsales@pearsontechgroup.com

For sales outside the U.S. please contact: **International Sales** international@pearsoned.com

CISCO SYSTEMS

Corporate Headquarters
Cisco Systems, Inc.
170 West Tasman Drive
San Jose, CA 95134-1706
USA
www.cisco.com
Tel: 408 526-4000
    800 553-NETS (6387)
Fax: 408 526-4100

European Headquarters
Cisco Systems International BV
Haarlerbergpark
Haarlerbergweg 13-19
1101 CH Amsterdam
The Netherlands
www-europe.cisco.com
Tel: 31 0 20 357 1000
Fax: 31 0 20 357 1100

Americas Headquarters
Cisco Systems, Inc.
170 West Tasman Drive
San Jose, CA 95134-1706
USA
www.cisco.com
Tel: 408 526-7660
Fax: 408 527-0883

Asia Pacific Headquarters
Cisco Systems, Inc.
Capital Tower
168 Robinson Road
#22-01 to #29-01
Singapore 068912
www.cisco.com
Tel: +65 6317 7777
Fax: +65 6317 7799

Cisco Systems has more than 200 offices in the following countries and regions. Addresses, phone numbers, and fax numbers are listed on the
Cisco.com Web site at www.cisco.com/go/offices.

Argentina • Australia • Austria • Belgium • Brazil • Bulgaria • Canada • Chile • China PRC • Colombia • Costa Rica • Croatia • Czech Republic
Denmark • Dubai, UAE • Finland • France • Germany • Greece • Hong Kong SAR • Hungary • India • Indonesia • Ireland • Israel • Italy
Japan • Korea • Luxembourg • Malaysia • Mexico • The Netherlands • New Zealand • Norway • Peru • Philippines • Poland • Portugal
Puerto Rico • Romania • Russia • Saudi Arabia • Scotland • Singapore • Slovakia • Slovenia • South Africa • Spain • Sweden
Switzerland • Taiwan • Thailand • Turkey • Ukraine • United Kingdom • United States • Venezuela • Vietnam • Zimbabwe

About the Author

Jim Geier is the founder and principal consultant of Wireless-Nets, Ltd. (www.wireless-nets.com), an independent consulting firm, which assists companies with the development and deployment of wireless LAN products and systems. His 20 years of experience include the analysis, design, software development, installation, and support of numerous client/server and wireless network-based systems for enterprises, airports, homes, retail stores, manufacturing facilities, warehouses, and hospitals throughout the world.

Jim is a voting member within the Wi-Fi Alliance, responsible for certifying interoperability of 802.11 (Wi-Fi) wireless LANs. He served as chairman of the IEEE Computer Society, Dayton Section, and chairman of the IEEE International Conference on Wireless LAN Implementation. He has been an active member of the IEEE 802.11 Working Group, responsible for developing international standards for wireless LANs. Jim is an advisory board member of several leading wireless LAN companies.

Jim is the author of several books including *Wireless LANs* (SAMS, ISBN: 0672320584), *Wireless Networking Handbook* (MTP, ISBN: 156205631X), and *Network Reengineering* (McGraw-Hill, ISBN: 007023034X), as well as numerous articles. He is also editor-in-chief of MobilizedSoftware.com, an online publication assisting developers with implementing mobile applications.

Jim's education includes a bachelor's and master's degree in electrical engineering and a master's degree in business administration.

Contact Jim Geier at jimgeier@wireless-nets.com.

About the Technical Reviewers

Joel Barrett is a wireless specialist with Cisco Systems. He has attained the Cisco CCNP, CCDP, and wireless specialization, as well as CWNA, MCSE, and Master CNE. Within Cisco, Joel is the team leader for the Channels Technology Advisory Team for Mobility, an advisor for the Enterprise Mobility Virtual Team, and a member of Cisco's Enterprise Mobility Technology Leadership Program. He is an advisor for the Wireless Technology Forum, and a coauthor and principle technical editor for wireless LAN technology books including *CWSP Official Study Guide* and *Managing and Securing a Cisco Structured Wireless-Aware Network*.

Joel and his wife, Barbara Kurth, live near Atlanta, Georgia with their two daughters and son. His personal website is http://www.brainslap.com/joel.

D. Ed Lamprecht is the manager of the Professional Services Group at Monarch Marking Systems, which focuses on custom software and network solutions. He has over 17 years of programming experience in applications, operating systems, and network programming. In 1988, Ed joined Monarch Marking Systems, a company specializing in bar code printers and labels. Since 1996, Ed has been involved in data-collection systems providing wireless network connectivity solutions of handheld printers and data collection terminals for retail, industrial, manufacturing, and health-care markets.

At Monarch, Ed has developed client/server applications, visited customer sites for analysis and problem solving, and provided international training on products and wireless connectivity. Ed holds seven patents in bar code software and handheld printer/data collectors.

Ed lives with his wife, Michelle, and his son, Colin, in Dayton, Ohio. When not tinkering with PCs and networks at home, he enjoys model railroading, railroad memorabilia collecting, golfing, traveling, and spending time with his family.

Joseph Roth is a Lieutenant Commander in the U.S. Navy currently serving as a military professor and Network Security Group department head at the Naval Postgraduate School (NPS). He holds four master's degrees: computer science

(NPS), information system technology (NPS), public administration (University of Maryland), and national security and strategic studies (Naval War College). Joseph also holds a bachelor's degree in computer engineering from George Washington University and two certificates of higher education from the University of Cambridge. He has obtained numerous industry certifications including CCNA, CWNA, Security +, Network +, and MCP. His articles have been published in *InfoWorld* and *Federal Computer Week*. Joseph served in Europe for five years and has been deployed to the Balkans and the Middle East.

Dedications

To Madison, Sierra, and Eric

Acknowledgments

I'd like to offer thanks to my son, Eric Geier, for assisting me with the research for this book. Eric is a member of the technical staff of my consulting company, Wireless-Nets, Ltd., where he researches and analyzes wireless network technologies, performs wireless LAN analysis, and develops computer-based training courses.

Eric is a Certified Wireless Network Professional (CWNP) and founder of www.wirelessnetworks4homes.com, a website focusing on the deployment of wireless LANs for homes and small offices.

Contents at a Glance

x

Contents

Introduction

For several decades, people have been using computer networks to interconnect personal computers and servers in companies, colleges, and cities. An evolution has been taking place, however, toward using networks wirelessly. In fact, today wireless interfaces are available to utilize network services that allow us to use e-mail and access applications, and browse the Internet from just about anywhere.

These wireless applications are enabling people to extend their workplace in a way that results in significant benefits. Business travelers, for example, are able to respond to e-mails while waiting for a flight at an airport. A homeowner can easily share a common Internet connection among multiple PCs and laptops without running cabling. This book explains the underlying technologies that make these types of applications possible.

Goals of This Book

The intent of this book is to offer a basic introduction to wireless network applications, components, and technologies. These concepts provide a solid basis for understanding various wireless network topics in more detail. After reading this book, you'll be able to effectively continue a study of specific wireless networks.

Who Ought to Read This Book

This book was written for anyone beginning a study of wireless networks. There is no need for readers to have a technical background. CEOs, managers, and business owners will benefit from reading this book, as will engineers and technicians. Even users wanting to understand the inner workings of wireless networks will find this book interesting.

How This Book Is Organized

This book covers all aspects of wireless networks, with emphasis on the unique attributes of wireless systems. The first three chapters provide the basic building blocks for a better understanding of the different types of wireless networks that the subsequent chapters describe. The final chapter offers details on securing wireless networks.

- **Chapter 1, "The Wireless World: An Introduction to Concepts"**—This chapter fully defines a wireless network and briefly defines the various types. Many examples of wireless network applications are given with discussion of resulting benefits.

- **Chapter 2, "Wireless System Architecture: How Wireless Works"**—This chapter offers a broad explanation of the various components of a wireless network. By illustrating how information flows through the network, this chapter provides an excellent basis for understanding how different types of wireless networks operate.

- **Chapter 3, "Radio Frequency and Light Signal Fundamentals: The Invisible Medium"**—This chapter details how radio frequency and light signals carry information through the air medium. These are the primary elements that define a wireless network.

- **Chapter 4, "Wireless PANs: Networks for Small Places"**—This chapter explains the components, technologies, and configurations of a wireless personal-area network (PAN).

- **Chapter 5, "Wireless LANs: Networks for Buildings and Campuses"**—This chapter explains the components, technologies, and configurations of a wireless local-area network (LAN).

- **Chapter 6, "Wireless MANs: Networks for Connecting Buildings and Remote Areas"**—This chapter explains the components, technologies, and configurations of a wireless metropolitan-area network (MAN).

- **Chapter 7, "Wireless WANs: Networks for Worldwide Connections Resources"**—This chapter explains the components, technologies, and configurations of a wireless wide-area network (WAN).

- **Chapter 8, "Wireless Network Security: Protecting Information Resources"**—This chapter describes potential security threats to and countermeasures for wireless networks. When installing a wireless network, security is important because of the nature of wireless signals.

- **Appendix A, "Answers to Chapter Review Questions"**—This appendix contains answers and explanations to the chapter review questions that appear at the end of each chapter.

- **Glossary**—The glossary is a tool that you can easily reference as you come across key terms throughout the book.

Stuff You'll Find in This Book

This book includes several features that should help you master wireless topics. Here's a summary of the elements that you'll find:

- **What You Will Learn**—Every chapter begins with a list of objectives that are addressed in the chapter. The objectives summarize what you will learn in the chapter.

- **Key terms and Glossary**—Throughout this book, you will see key terms formatted with bold and italics. These terms are particularly significant in wireless networking. So, if you find you aren't familiar with the term or at any point need a refresher, just look up the term in the Glossary toward the end of the book to find a full definition.

- **Chapter summaries**—Every chapter concludes with a comprehensive chapter summary that reviews chapter objectives, ensuring complete coverage and discussing the chapter's relationship to future content.

- **Chapter review questions**—Every chapter concludes with review questions. These questions test the basic ideas and concepts covered in each chapter. You can find the answers and explanations to the questions in Appendix A.

■ **Nontechie headings and explanations**—The headings and text used throughout this book avoid the use of technical terms when possible, focusing instead on words that connote something about the underlying concepts.

The illustrations in this book use the following icons for networking devices and connections:

Printer

Mobile Phone

Laptop

Base Station,
Access Point,
or Router

Desktop PC

Bridge

Personal
Digital
Assistant

Broadband
Modem

What You Will Learn

After reading this chapter, you should be able to

- ✔ Compare and contrast wireless PANs, LANs, MANs, and WANs

- ✔ Recognize general examples of wireless network applications

- ✔ Understand the benefits of wireless networks

CHAPTER 1

The Wireless World: An Introduction to Concepts

Wireless networks play a crucial role in the lives of people at work, home, and public places. Even though a wireless network has a simple purpose, which is to provide connections between users and information sources without the use of wires, critical concepts of wireless networks must be mastered before understanding how they operate. This chapter presents a thorough definition of wireless networks and how they benefit users in different applications.

Wireless Networks Defined

A wireless network enables people to communicate and access applications and information without wires. This provides freedom of movement and the ability to extend applications to different parts of a building, city, or nearly anywhere in the world. For example, people at home researching on the Internet can do so in a quiet area away from noisy children or in front of the television with the entire family nearby. Wireless networks allow people to interact with e-mail or browse the Internet from a location that they prefer.

Wireless networks have been around for many years. In fact, early forms of wireless communications include Native Americans waving buffalo skins over a fire to send smoke signals to others over great distances. Also, the use of pulsing lights carrying information through Morse code between ships has been and still is an important form of communications. Of course, cell phones are also a type of wireless communication and are popular today for people talking to each other worldwide.

Many types of wireless communication systems exist, but a distinguishing attribute of a wireless network is that communication takes place between computer devices. These devices include *personal digital assistants (PDAs)*, laptops, personal computers (PCs), servers, and printers. Computer devices have processors, memory, and a means of interfacing with a particular type of network. Traditional cell phones don't fall within the definition of a computer device; however, newer phones and even audio headsets are beginning to incorporate computing power and network adapters. Eventually, most electronics will offer wireless network connections.

As with networks based on wire, or *optical fiber*, wireless networks convey information between computer devices. The information can take the form of e-mail messages, web pages, database records, streaming video or voice. In most cases, wireless networks transfer *data*, such as e-mail messages and files, but advancements in the performance of wireless networks is enabling support for video and voice communications as well.

As discussed in Chapter 3, "Radio Frequency and Light Signal Fundamentals: The Invisible Medium," wireless networks use either radio waves or infrared light as a medium for communication between users, servers, and databases. This type of communication is invisible to the human eye. In addition, the actual medium (air) is transparent to the user. Most manufacturers are now integrating the wireless network interface card (NIC; also referred to as an adapter) and antenna into computing devices and out of view from the user. This makes wireless computing devices mobile and easy to use.

Wireless networks fall into several categories, depending on the size of the physical area that they are capable of covering. The following types of wireless networks satisfy diverse user requirements:

- Wireless Personal-Area Network (PAN)

- Wireless Local-Area Network (LAN)

- Wireless Metropolitan-Area Network (MAN)

- Wireless Wide-Area Network (WAN)

These terms are merely an extension of the more basic forms of wired networks (such as LAN or WAN) that have been in use for years before wireless networks came about.

Table 1-1 shows a brief comparison of these forms of wireless networks. Each type of wireless network has complementary attributes that satisfy different requirements. The subsequent sections briefly explore each wireless network.

Table 1-1   Comparison of Wireless Network Types

Type	Coverage	Performance	Standards	Applications
Wireless PAN	Within reach of a person	Moderate	Bluetooth, IEEE 802.15, and IrDa	Cable replacement for peripherals
Wireless LAN	Within a building or campus	High	IEEE 802.11, Wi-Fi, and HiperLAN	Mobile extension of wired networks
Wireless MAN	Within a city	High	Proprietary, IEEE 802.16, and WIMAX	Fixed wireless between homes and businesses and the Internet
Wireless WAN	Worldwide	Low	CDPD and Cellular 2G, 2.5G, and 3G	Mobile access to the Internet from outdoor areas

Wireless PANs

As Figure 1-1 illustrates, wireless PANs have relatively short range (up to 50 feet) and are most effective for fulfilling requirements within a small room or personal area. The performance of wireless PANs is moderate, with *data rates* up to 2 Mbps. These attributes satisfy needs for replacing cables in many situations.

Wireless PAN Enables the Interconnection of Computer
Devices Within Close Reach of the User

A wireless PAN, for example, might involve someone wirelessly synchronizing
his PDA to a laptop or desktop computer. Likewise, a wireless PAN can provide
wireless connectivity to a printer. The benefit of eliminating the tangle of wires
when using computer peripherals in this fashion is extremely useful, and the initial installation and movement of peripherals is easy.

The low power consumption and small footprint of most wireless PAN *transceivers*
make it possible to effectively support small user devices equipped with computer
processors. The lower power consumption allows the computer device to operate
over long periods of time without draining its battery. This, of course, avoids the
need for the user to charge batteries often.

The low power consumption, for example, leads to successful implementation of
wireless PANs in cell phones, PDAs, and audio headsets. The phone can continuously interface with the address book in the PDA so that all phone numbers in a
person's contact manager are available when making phone calls. The user can
also use a wireless headset when making phone calls, or listen to digital music
playing on the PDA. This avoids hooking wires on things while working or playing.

In addition, some wireless PANs can interconnect laptops and desktop PCs for the purpose of sharing Internet connections and applications. This might be suitable for a network within the confines of a room. Wireless LANs, however, consist of attributes that better support building-wide wireless connectivity.

Most wireless PANs use radio waves for carrying information through air. For example, the **Bluetooth** specification defines the operation of a wireless PAN operating in the 2.4-GIIz frequency band with a range of 50 feet and data rates up to 2 Mbps. Furthermore, the Institute of Electrical and Electronic Engineers (IEEE) **802.15** standard incorporates the Bluetooth specification for wireless PANs. These technologies offer a reliable, long-term solution for connecting computer devices within a small area.

Some wireless PANs employ infrared light to carry information from one point to another. The Infrared Data Association (IrDA) specification defines the use of direct infrared beams to provide ranges of up to three feet and data rates as high as 4 Mbps. The advantage of infrared light is freedom from radio frequency interference, but the line-of-sight requirement between computer devices limits the placement of wireless components. An office partition, for example, blocks the path of the infrared light signal, which reduces the usability of the wireless device to a small area.

note
Refer to Chapter 4, "Wireless PANs: Networks for Small Places," for details on wireless PAN technologies and products.

Wireless LANs

Wireless LANs supply high performance within and around office buildings, factories, and homes. (See Figure 1-2.) Users in these areas typically have laptops, PCs, and PDAs with large screens and processors that support higher-end applications. Wireless LANs efficiently satisfy connectivity requirements for these types of computer devices.

Figure 1-2   A Wireless LAN Enables the Interconnection of Computer Devices Within the Confines of a Building

A business, for example, can install a wireless LAN to offer mobile access to corporate applications from laptops. With this type of system, a user can utilize network services from conference rooms and other places while away from their office. This allows employees to be more efficient while working away from their desks and collaborating with others.

Wireless LANs easily provide levels of performance that enable the higher-end applications to run smoothly. For example, wireless LAN users can easily view a large e-mail attachment or stream video from a server. With data rates of up to 54 Mbps, a wireless LAN can satisfy just about any office or home network application.

Wireless LANs are similar to traditional wired *Ethernet* LANs in their performance, components, costs, and operation.

Because of the widespread implementation of wireless LAN adapters in laptops, most public wireless network providers deploy wireless LANs to provide mobile, broadband access to the Internet. Users within range of a public wireless LAN at a hotspot, such as an airport or hotel, can access e-mail and browse the Internet for a fee (if the faculty doesn't offer it for free). The rapid growth rate of public wireless LANs is making the Internet available to people at areas where people tend to congregate.

IEEE *802.11* is the most prevalent standard for wireless LANs, with versions operating in the 2.4-GHz and 5-GHz frequency bands. A problem with 802.11 is that there is limited interoperability among various versions of the standard. For example, a wireless LAN computer device using 802.11a adapters will not connect with another computer device that implements 802.11b. In addition, there are other issues with the 802.11 standard, such as limited security, which is discussed in later chapters of this book.

In order to solve issues with the 802.11 standard, the Wi-Fi Alliance incorporates assorted functions of 802.11 into a standard they refer to as *Wireless Fidelity (Wi-Fi)*. If a wireless LAN product complies with Wi-Fi, there are assurances that the product is interoperable with other Wi-Fi products. The additional openness of Wi-Fi ensures that diverse users can operate on the same wireless LAN. This is extremely important with public wireless LANs.

note
Refer to Chapter 5, "Wireless LANs: Networks for Buildings and Campuses," for details on wireless LAN technologies and products.

Wireless MANs

Wireless MANs encompass areas the size of cities. In most cases, applications involve fixed connectivity, but some implementations enable mobility. For example, a hospital can deploy a wireless MAN to provide data communications between the main hospital facility and a remote clinic. Or, a power utility company can install a wireless MAN throughout a city to supply access to work orders from various sites. As a result, wireless MANs can connect existing network infrastructures together or allow mobile users to communicate with an existing network infrastructure.

Wireless Internet Service Providers (WISPs) provide wireless MANs in cities and rural areas, as Figure 1-3 illustrates, to provide fixed wireless connections for homes and companies. A wireless MAN offers significant advantages when traditional wired connections (such as Digital Subscriber Line [DSL] and cable modem) are not feasible to install. Wireless MANs are effective when right-of-way restrictions make wired systems impossible or too expensive.

Figure 1-3   Wireless MAN Is an Alterative for Homes and Companies Needing to Connect to an Internet Service

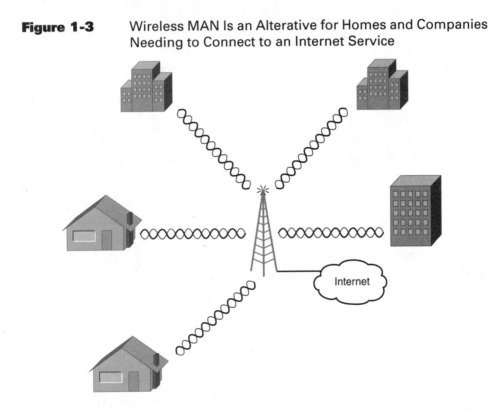

Wireless MAN performance varies. Connections between buildings using infrared light can reach 100 Gbps or more; whereas radio links over a 20-mile distance

might provide only 100 kbps. The actual performance depends on the choice from a wide assortment of technologies and components.

Many proprietary wireless MAN solutions are on the market, but the industry is beginning to settle on the use of standards. Some vendors utilize the IEEE 802.11 standard as the basis for wireless MANs. While the use of 802.11 systems is optimum for satisfying requirements within buildings, 802.11 solutions can connect buildings over metropolitan distances using antennae that focus transmission and reception of the signals in one direction.

A greater number of companies are now beginning to deploy IEEE 802.16 systems, a relatively new standard with products just becoming available. 802.16 offers a standardized solution for deploying effective wireless MANs with performance in the megabits-per-second range over appreciable ranges. As a result, 802.16 will likely become a common standard for wireless MANs.

note
Refer to Chapter 6, "Wireless MANs: Networks for Connecting Buildings and Remote Areas," for details on wireless MAN technologies and products.

Wireless WANs

Wireless WANs offer mobile applications covering a large area, such as a country or continent. Because of economies of scale, a telecommunications operator can feasibly deploy the relatively expensive wireless WAN infrastructure to provide long-range connectivity for a large customer base. The costs such as deployment can be spread across many users, resulting in low subscriber fees.

Wireless WANs, as Figure 1-4 indicates, have nearly worldwide coverage through the cooperation of multiple telecommunications companies. Well-established roaming agreements among telecommunications operators enable continuous connections for instant mobile data communications. By paying one telecommunications service provider, a user can access limited Internet services over a wireless WAN from almost anywhere in the world.

Figure 1-4   A Wireless WAN Is Capable of Supporting Mobile
Applications over a Wide Area

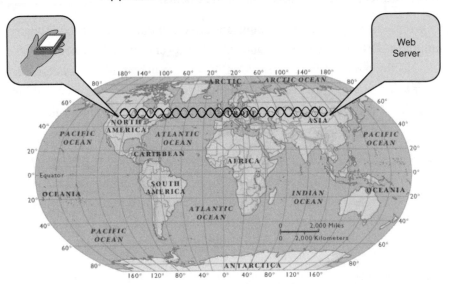

Performance of wireless WANs is relatively low, with data rates of up to 170 kbps
and typical rates of 56 kbps. This level of performance is similar to dial-up telephone modems. Special web portals, however, made to streamline information
content work efficiently with smaller devices and lower performance networks.
This makes the most from the limited bandwidth of wireless WANs.

The per-user data rates of wireless WANs are relatively low, but that is generally
acceptable because of the small devices (for example, cell phones and PDAs) that
people carry with them in situations where they need wireless WAN connectivity.
The smaller screen sizes and limited processing power of cell phones do not
require high performance. The transmission of video to a small cell phone or PDA
screen can be done with lower data rates.

Wireless WAN applications involve users accessing the Internet, sending and
receiving e-mails, and accessing corporate applications while away from the
home and office. Subscribers to wireless WAN services, for example, can stay
connected while traveling in taxis or walking throughout a city. A wireless WAN

can reach more places than other types of wireless networks, enabling users to carry on business and leisure activities from many different locations.

Wireless WANs include several competing standards that are slowly evolving. For example, ***Cellular Digital Packet Data (CDPD)*** is an older technology that enables the transmission of data over analog cell phone systems with data rates of 19.2 kbps. Some companies still offer CDPD in the U.S., but it is becoming obsolete as telecommunication operators move toward Third Generation (3G) telecommunications systems, with data rates possible in the megabit-per-second range.

An issue with the deployment of wireless WAN technology is it does not lend itself to coverage inside facilities, such as homes, offices, airports, and convention centers. Because wireless WAN infrastructure is outdoors, the radio signals of wireless WANs lose most of their strength when penetrating a facility. As a result, wireless WAN users within buildings might have poor performance and possibly no connectivity at all. Some telecommunications companies install wireless WAN systems within buildings, but this is expensive and is not feasible in most situations.

note
Refer to Chapter 7, "Wireless WANs: Networks for Worldwide Connections," for details on wireless WAN technologies and products.

Drawing the Line

Wireless PANs, LANs, MANs, and WANs are complementary and satisfy different types of requirements. Sometimes, however, it is difficult to distinguish one type from the other. For example, a wireless LAN within a building can provide connectivity between a person's PDA and PC, similar to that provided by a wireless PAN.

Technologies and standards, though, clearly differentiate one wireless network from another. Wireless PANs predominately use IEEE 802.15 (or Bluetooth), wireless LANs use IEEE 802.11 (or Wi-Fi), and so on. The key when deploying wireless networks is to fully define system requirements and choose the type that does the best job of satisfying requirements.

In terms of the user perspective, wireless networks are blending together. NICs for computer devices that support multiple wireless networks are becoming available. A traveler, for example, might have an advanced cell phone that interfaces with both wireless LANs and wireless WANs. This enables a seamless, wireless connection as the person interfaces with e-mail while roaming inside an airport using a public wireless LAN or travels in a taxi to a hotel while interfacing with one of the cellular-based data services.

Wireless Network Applications

Wireless networks support many applications that benefit from user mobility and higher reliability because of less error-prone cabling. Furthermore, many wireless network applications realize significant cost savings because of increases in efficiencies and less downtime as compared to a wired network. Most wireless network technologies are license free, making them simple and cost effective to deploy.

Basic Configurations

In most cases, the wireless network is merely an extension of an existing wired network. In this case, a user is able to perform a particular task at an optimum location instead of somewhere that is less than ideal. A clerk unloading a truck, for example, can use a wireless handheld unit to scan items that the clerk removes from the truck. This is much more effective than writing down the item numbers and later entering them at a desktop terminal located somewhere inside the facility and far away from the loading dock.

Other situations involve dedicated wireless networks, which completely eliminate the need for wiring. For example, an emergency team responding to an airplane crash scene can quickly establish a temporary wireless network within the immediate area of the crash. All computer devices communicate directly with each other. This makes it possible for team members to have centralized access to important data concerning the crash.

Applications of wireless networks also fall within private or public scenarios. A company or homeowner that purchases and installs a wireless network for its own use is enabling a private application. Usually, private applications are made only available for company employees or home occupants. Access to the applications is not made available to the general public. In fact, companies generally implement security safeguards to ensure that only authorized people can connect to the network and access services.

Public applications, on the other hand, provide open access to anyone. A business traveler, for example, can use a public wireless LAN at an airport to access the Internet while waiting for a flight. These public hotspots are becoming widely available in airports and other areas, such as hotels, convention centers, and coffee shops where there are large concentrations of people toting computer devices.

Internet Access

One of the most compelling reasons to install a wireless network is to enable the sharing of a single high-speed Internet connection. With this type of configuration, every member of a family or small business can easily share a single high-speed connection that a cable or DSL modem offers. This is convenient and saves money because everybody can simultaneously have access to the Internet and roam anywhere in the house or office.

The wireless network in this scenario also increases the flexibility of the network because it's easy to add new workstations at any time without having to run cable. The relocation of wireless PCs, along with any printers and servers, is also painless.

A company can implement a wireless network to allow visiting employees and guests with wireless computer devices to quickly connect to the network with little configuration. The ability to use the Internet while away from the home location can greatly enhance productivity. The visitor can just turn on their laptop and have instant access to e-mail and applications.

Voice over Wireless

The use of wireless networks to support the transmission of voice conversations is a beneficial solution when people need to constantly stay in contact with each other. In fact, a wireless LAN designed to support voice communications can completely replace a traditional wire-based telephone system within a particular facility. (See Figure 1-5.) The combination of voice and data over the same wireless network provides total mobility and lower operating costs.

Figure 1-5   Wireless LAN Provides the Infrastructure for a Telephone System Within a Building

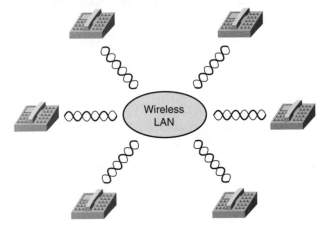

For example, employees within a retail store can locate certain clothes for a customer or check inventory by using special wireless LAN phones. The wireless LAN in the retail store can also support the transmission of bar codes when performing inventory or pricing using a wireless, handheld bar code scanner. Cost savings result because the company needs only to install and support a single communications system that carries both voice and data.

Likewise, a business can deploy their entire telephone system over a wireless LAN. This enables employees to carry their phone with them at all times, similar to a standard cell phone. Employees can accept calls within the facility at any time using a single phone.

Inventory Control

Many businesses profit from using wireless LANs when managing their manufacturing processes. This lowers operating costs. Because the connections between the manufacturing equipment and main control systems are wireless, the company can reconfigure the assembly process at any time from anywhere, saving time and money.

Through the use of a wireless LAN, a company can track and update inventory in real time, enabling efficiency and accuracy to increase dramatically. In a retail environment, as soon as a clerk purchases or stocks a product, a wireless management solution can update the inventory. In a manufacturing setting, the company can keep the raw materials and finished product statistics up-to-date. Employees equipped with wireless-enabled bar code scanners can check or change product prices or check the number in stock.

The improved accuracy provided by using a wireless LAN to manage inventory creates a chain reaction of benefits. Because the clerks enter the information directly into the main computer through handheld scanners, there is no paperwork to deal with. This significantly reduces human error when entering data, which leads to accurate financial records. This is important to manufacturing companies because accurate financial records ensure correct taxes are paid and fines (and possible law suits) are kept to a minimum.

Health Care

More and more hospitals are deploying wireless networks to improve operational efficiency and convenience. In most cases, hospitals deploy wireless LANs in high patient-traffic areas including emergency rooms, critical care wards, nursing stations, as well as in doctor's offices and patient waiting areas. Hospital staff can use mobile computer devices to increase efficiency and accuracy when caring for patients.

Health-care centers must maintain accurate records to ensure quality patient care. A simple mistake can cost someone's life. As a result, doctors and nurses must carefully record test results, physical data, pharmaceutical orders, and surgical procedures. This paperwork often overwhelms health-care staff, taking 50-70 percent of their time. The use of a mobile data collection device that wirelessly transmits the data to a centralized database significantly increases accuracy and raises the visibility of the data to those who need the information.

Doctors and nurses are also extremely mobile, going from room to room caring for patients. The use of electronic patient records, with the ability to input, view, and update patient data from anywhere in the hospital, increases the accuracy and speed of health care. This improvement is possible by providing each nurse and doctor with a wireless pen-based computer, such as a tablet or PDA, coupled with a wireless network to databases that store critical medical information about the patients.

A doctor caring for someone in the hospital, for example, can place an order for a blood test by keying the request into a handheld computer. The laboratory receives the order electronically and dispatches a lab technician to draw blood from the patient. The laboratory runs the tests requested by the doctor and enter the results into the patient's electronic medical record. The doctor can then check the results via the handheld appliance from anywhere in the hospital.

Another hospital application is tracking of pharmaceuticals. The use of mobile handheld bar code printing and scanning devices dramatically increases the efficiency and accuracy of all drug transactions, such as receiving, picking, dispensing, inventory, and expiration dates. Most importantly, however, it ensures that hospital staff can administer the right drug to the right person in a timely fashion.

Education

Many colleges and elementary schools are finding beneficial reasons to install wireless LANs, mostly to provide mobile network applications to their students. In fact, schools have begun using the existence of wireless LAN access as a competitive advantage. These schools are targeting the growing number of students with laptops and expectations of accessing the Internet and school resources from anywhere on campus, such as classrooms, libraries, quads, and dormitories. Students are able to readily check e-mail, surf the Web, access specialized school applications, check grades, and view transcripts. As a result, students make better use of their time.

It's expensive to establish and maintain computer labs for students to utilize for accessing the Internet and completing assignments. Students must often wait in line for using a computer in a lab, which cuts into other activities. A wireless LAN, however, gives students access to needed resources using their own laptop from anywhere on campus at any time, even after the traditional computer lab closes. This more evenly distributes network access to all students, enhancing student efficiency. Of course, the school can also save the costs of running the computer lab.

Real Estate

Real estate salespeople perform a great deal of their work away from the office, usually talking with customers at the property being sold or rented. Before leaving the office, salespeople normally identify a few sites to show a customer, print the Multiple Listing Service (MLS) information that describes the property, and then drive to each location with the potential buyer. If the customer is unhappy with that round of sites, the real estate agent must drive back to the office and run more listings. Even if the customer decides to purchase the property, they must both go back to the real estate office to finish paperwork that completes the sale.

Wireless networking makes the sale of real estate much more efficient. The real estate agent can use a computer away from the office to access a wireless MLS record. An agent can also use a portable computer and printer to produce contracts and loan applications for signing at the point of sale.

Utilities

Utility companies operate and maintain a highly distributed system that delivers power and natural gas to industries and residences. Utility companies must continually monitor the operation of the electrical distribution system, gas lines, and water consumption, and must check usage meters at least monthly to calculate bills. Traditionally, this means a person must travel from location to location, visit residences and company facilities, record information, and then enter the data at a service or computing center.

Today, utility companies employ wireless WANs to support the automation of meter reading and system monitoring. Instead of a meter reader recording the data on a sheet of paper to later enter in a computer for processing, the meter can periodically transmit the data through the wireless WAN to the utility company. This saves time and reduces overhead costs by eliminating the need for human meter readers.

Field Service

Field service personnel spend most of their time on the road installing and maintaining systems or inspecting facilities under construction. To complete their jobs, these individuals need access to product documentation and procedures. Traditionally, field service employees have had to carry several binders of documentation with them to sites that often lacked a phone and even electricity.

In some cases, the field person might not be able to take all the documents to a job site, causing delay while obtaining the proper information. On long trips, this information might also become outdated. Updates require delivery that might take days to reach the person in the field. Wireless WAN access to documentation can definitely enhance field service. A field service employee, for example, can carry a portable computer that connects to the office LAN that contains accurate documentation of all applicable information.

Field Sales

Sales professionals are always on the move and meeting with customers. While on site with a customer, a salesperson needs access to vast information that describes products and services. Salespeople must also place orders, provide status—such as meeting schedules—to the home office, and maintain inventories.

With wireless access to the main office network, a salesperson can view centralized contact information, retrieve product information, produce proposals, create contracts, and stay in touch with office staff and other salespeople. This contact permits salespeople to complete the entire sale directly from the customer site, which increases the potential for a successful sale and shortens the sales cycle.

Vending

Beverage and snack companies place vending machines in hotels, airports, and office buildings to enhance the sales of their products. Vending machines eliminate the need for a human salesclerk. These companies, however, must send employees around to stock the machines periodically. In some cases, machines might become empty before the restocking occurs because the company has no way of knowing when the machine runs out of a particular product.

A wireless WAN can support the monitoring of stock levels by transporting applicable data from each of the vending machines to a central database that can be easily viewed by company personnel from a single location. Such monitoring allows companies to be proactive in stocking their machines, because they always know the stock levels at each machine. This enables the vending company to schedule appropriate stops for people who refill the machines.

Public Networks

Because of the significant proliferation of laptops, PDAs, and cell phones, a growing need exists for mobile interfaces to the Internet and corporate applications. Users want and expect seamless, constant mobile connectivity to all information sources with high levels of performance and availability. Wireless networks provide the infrastructure to support these needs in public areas that are away from the home or office.

A public wireless network offers a means for people on the go to connect with the Internet. In general, the places that have large groups of people that need or want network connections have wireless LAN access. Wireless MANs and WANs, on the other hand, provide coverage over larger areas having sparsely distributed populations.

Public wireless LANs are in common places such as hotels and restaurants, but all kinds of places are installing wireless LANs for public access. For example, approximately 90 percent of all boaters use the Internet regularly while at home or in the office. Many still want access to the Internet while relaxing on their boats, especially when parked overnight at a marina. As a result, marinas around the globe are installing wireless LANs to enable boaters to have access to Internet applications.

 note
Refer to the following website for an extensive list of public wireless LANs: http://www.wi-fihotspotlist.com/.

To use a public wireless LAN, users must have a computer device, such as a laptop, with a wireless LAN NIC. IEEE 802.11b (Wi-Fi) is the most common type of wireless LAN today that public wireless network providers install. The computer device's NIC automatically senses the presence of the wireless LAN and associates with the network. Before accessing the Internet, the user must subscribe to the service, generally through a website accessible from the wireless LAN. Some public wireless LANs are free, but most providers charge a nominal price for using the service.

Another form of public wireless network uses wireless MAN technologies to provide wireless communications links between subscribers (homes and offices) and the Internet. The provider mounts a small antenna dish on the home or small office and points it to a centralized hub. This point-to-multipoint system provides the last-mile connection necessary to supply Internet access to locations where DSL and cable modem connections are not available or feasible.

Location-Based Services

With wireless networks, you can make the location of a particular person or item available to a central location. The ability to track the position of moving objects brings about some interesting applications. The coordinates of users can feed into a server-based application that implements a location-based service.

For example, a public wireless LAN provider can use this concept to display pertinent information to travelers as they walk through an airport or train station. Information might include their location on a moving map, in a way that the passenger can use to find the way to the next departure gate or the nearest restaurant. The value of this location-based service could entice passengers to use the particular venue.

A hospital might use *location-based services* to track the positions of doctors and nurses. This enables hospital administrators to dispatch the right person to an emergency. Patients end up receiving more rapid and effective care.

The usage of location-aware systems over wireless LANs is also moving to the consumer market. For example, the ability to track children is extremely valuable. Imagine being in a theme park and a toddler wandering off without the knowledge of the parent. With a location system, the parent can easily find the toddler among a large crowd. With a concealed wireless tracking tag located on the child, this type of system can aid tremendously if someone kidnaps a child.

A shopping mall might deploy a location system and send electronic flyers and advertisements to customers carrying PDAs. The system takes into consideration the physical location of shoppers within the facility and customizes actual content appropriately. Shoppers then make better use of their time, and stores make more money.

Users in this example might receive an electronic directory and advertisement flyer on their wireless PDA after entering the mall. The directory includes a map of the facility that identifies the person's exact position. As the shopper clicks on a store, restroom, or ATM in the directory, the map indicates directions that take them to the desired selection. If a spouse or shopping friend is carrying a wireless device, everyone can keep track of each other's location as well.

Wireless Network Benefits

People worldwide are learning of the benefits of wireless connectivity for checking e-mail, browsing the Internet, and accessing corporate applications. Ongoing advances in products that include wireless interfaces enable these people to unwire and reap the benefits of mobility and flexibility. The outcomes are higher efficiencies, accuracies, and reliability.

Increasing Efficiency and Accuracy

For compelling reasons to install a wireless network, strongly consider continual productivity benefits. If benefits result in enough savings to counter the costs associated with installing and supporting a wireless network, a wireless network is beneficial. A positive return on investment certainly motivates people to allocate money for new systems.

Office Example

As the basis for increasing productivity, consider purchasing 802.11-equipped laptops. This enables employees to read and respond to e-mail and browse the Internet during office meetings, assuming the users can be responsive when needed at the meeting while plunking away at their laptop. Even though this seems trivial, the productivity gains can be significant.

If a user attends meetings for 3 hours each day and spends approximately 15 minutes per hour responding to e-mail and performing other Internet-related tasks during each meeting, the user has 45 minutes more each day to do other tasks. This seems pretty reasonable, considering the average person and office setting.

A 45-minute productivity gain equates to company cost savings that depend on the person's cost per hour. At $50 per hour, the savings is $37.50 per person per day. A smaller company with 20 users will save $750 per day, $15,000 per month, $180,000 per year, and so on. After including wireless LAN hardware costs of $40,000, a positive return could result in approximately three months! Even after factoring in the cost of new laptops for everyone, a company should still see a positive return in less than one year in this simple example.

In addition to gains in productivity, wireless networks offer the following benefits in offices:

- Users can continue networking when the company moves walls during facility remodeling, which frequently occurs in corporations.

- Visiting employees can easily network with company servers and applications from anywhere within the facility.

- The company can implement additional wireless applications, such as mobile phones, in order to save costs.

Warehouse Example

Mobility provides the basis for getting jobs done faster and with fewer people. Imagine a shipment of auto parts arriving at a distribution center. As clerks unload the trucks, they scan a bar code on each box with a wireless, handheld data collector. The bar code contains a unique tracking number that is automatically and immediately sent to a warehouse management system (WMS) to indicate the reception of the part. The WMS then instructs the clerks, through the data collector's display, whether to place the item in the warehouse or ship the item directly to a particular customer.

If the part is bound for the warehouse, the system prints a label for placement on the box identifying the intended storage position in the warehouse. The system prints route and shipping information on a label, which the clerks affix to the box for parts requiring shipment to a customer. The clerks can then deliver the box to the correct location, whether it's the warehouse or an outgoing delivery truck.

The use of this receiving system enables the company to reduce inventories by immediately redirecting received orders to customers. It also eliminates paper records and manual data entry. Most importantly, the company delivers orders to customers sooner. In general, the system enables a company to realize incredible gains in efficiency and accuracy over error-prone, paper-based processes. The tracking of items by paper and the entry of data to the WMS through a desktop terminal significantly increase the likelihood of errors and require larger staffs to accomplish.

Hospital Example

In a hospital, a wireless network can help save lives by improving the speed and accuracy of delivering drugs to patients. Because of government regulations, hospitals must maintain accurate records of narcotics, which prompts administrators to implement stringent, often paper-based, methods to account for the exact numbers of each narcotic. A wireless network, however, enables the use of handheld bar code scanners that make the picking and inventory process up to 300 percent faster and much more accurate.

In addition, a nurse can verify that the correct patient receives the medication by scanning both the drug and the patient's identification bracelet. This significantly reduces the chance of giving the drug to the wrong patient. In addition, the system can verify that the patient doesn't have any adverse allergies for the type of drug that she is receiving. The wireless network makes this application possible in a highly mobile hospital environment.

Many other applications result in enough gains in efficiencies and accuracies to make a wireless network worthwhile. The goal is to carefully quantify and compare the benefits to the system costs.

Improving Reliability

Cables are inherently unreliable because of corrosion and misuse. Improper installation and damage of cables are primary reasons that wired networks fail. A telephone technician, for example, might be repairing a problem with the telephone system and inadvertently cut network cables. This causes system downtime for a relatively long period while network administrators troubleshoot.

Adverse weather, such as hurricanes and tornadoes, can offer major harm to both aerial and underground copper connections between buildings. This type of damage frequently blocks an entire building from accessing important applications. Even though wired networks generally deliver higher performance than wireless counterparts, the susceptibility to outages results in unacceptable availability.

A wireless network appreciably reduces problems related to physical damage. The availability of the system increases, giving users connectivity a higher percentage of time. A wired network might be necessary if it's not possible to meet performance requirements with a wireless network, but a wireless network can provide a back-up link. The combination of wired and wireless communications linkage between buildings offers a reliable high-performance and system.

Chapter Summary

A wireless network eliminates wiring among computer devices, such as PDAs and laptops, and existing networks. This permits computer devices and users to be highly mobile while still interfacing with the Internet and corporate applications. Whether someone is within an airport, home, or office, the person can stay connected.

The various types of wireless networks offer solutions for a variety of applications in homes, offices, hospitals, and public areas, where users can benefit from having mobile access to network services. The ability to merely enable mobile applications is often enough justification for a wireless network. In some cases, however, a company might need to carefully analyze potential gains in efficiency, accuracy, and reliability to show that the costs of the system will be worthwhile.

Chapter Review Questions

You can find the answers to the following questions in Appendix A, "Answers to Chapter Review Questions."

1. What is a distinguishing attribute of a wireless network as compared to a general wireless communication system?

2. What types of information does a wireless network support?

3. What are the four types of wireless networks?

4. What is the typical maximum range of a wireless PAN?

5. True or false: A wireless PAN consumes little power from small handheld computer devices.

6. What is a common standard for wireless LANs?

7. What relatively new standard applies to wireless MANs?

8. Why do wireless WANs not effectively satisfy requirements for indoor wireless networks?

9. What is a common application of wireless networks in homes and small offices?

10. What are examples of applications for wireless WANs?

What You Will Learn

After reading this chapter, you should be able to

- ✔ Understand the components of a wireless network

- ✔ Discover general wireless network architectural elements

- ✔ Understand how information flows through a wireless network

CHAPTER 2

Wireless System Architecture: How Wireless Works

Wireless networks utilize components similar to wired networks; however, wireless networks must convert information signals into a form suitable for transmission through the air *medium*. Even though wireless networks directly contribute only to a portion of the overall network infrastructure, attention to all network functions is necessary to counter impairments resulting from the wireless medium. This chapter discusses concepts common to all types of wireless networks, with emphasis on components and information signals.

Wireless Network System Components

A wireless network consists of several components that support communications using radio or light waves propagating through an air medium. Some of these elements overlap with those of wired networks, but special consideration is necessary for all of these components when deploying a wireless network. Figure 2-1 illustrates these primary components.

Figure 2-1 Wireless Networks Include Computer Devices, Base Stations, and a Wireless Infrastructure

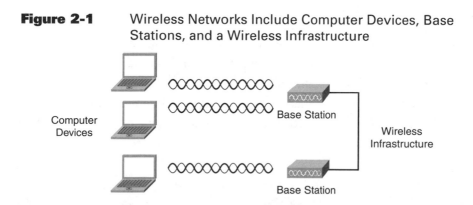

Users

A user can be anything that directly utilizes the wireless network. One of the most common types of user is a person. For example, a business traveler accessing the Internet from a public wireless LAN at an airport is a user. In some cases, however, the user might not be human. A robot, for example, might receive instructions over a wireless network from a central computer that controls a manufacturing process. Because the wireless network exists to serve the user, the user is the component that receives the benefits of a wireless network. As a result, users are an important part of the wireless network.

The user initiates and terminates use of a wireless network, making the term enduser appropriate. Typically, a user operates a *computer device*, which often performs a variety of application-specific functions in addition to offering an interface to the wireless network.

Users of wireless networks tend to be mobile, constantly moving throughout a facility, campus, or city. Mobility is one of the most prominent benefits of deploying a wireless network. For example, a person walking through a convention center while sending and receiving e-mail from a PDA is exercising mobility. The PDA in this case must have continual or frequent connections to a wireless network infrastructure.

Some users might require only portability; whereby, they stay at a particular location while using the wireless network for a specific period of time. An example of this type of usage is someone operating a laptop wirelessly from a conference room. The user will turn on the laptop after sitting down in the conference room and shut off the laptop before leaving. As a result, the wireless network doesn't need to support continual movement.

Other users might actually be stationary, which means that they operate from one place for an indefinite period of time. An example of this type of user is someone working from a wireless computer in an office. The biggest difference between a stationary and portable user is that the stationary user will not require any form of roaming functions. Roaming functions are difficult to implement in some situations.

Computer Devices

Many types of computer devices, sometimes referred to as clients, operate on a wireless network. Some computer devices might be specifically designed for users, whereas some computer devices are end systems. In generally, any computer device might communicate with any other computer device on the same wireless network. Figure 2-2 illustrates an assortment of computer devices for wireless networks.

Figure 2-2   Computer Devices for Wireless Networks Satisfy Different Applications

To support mobile applications, computer devices are often small, making them practical for people to carry with them at all times. These devices generally have small screens, limited keyboards, and small batteries. The devices are mobile, but they can support only certain applications.

With portable and stationary applications, however, the computer devices are much larger. These devices generally have larger displays and keyboards, making them more suitable to use when browsing the Internet and other applications requiring relatively high performance. The problem, however, is that these devices weigh more and are difficult to carry from one place to another.

Computer devices within a wireless network also include end systems such as servers, databases, and websites. For example, the http://www.cnn.com website includes news that someone can view from a public wireless LAN connection from a hotel room. Similarly, a clerk can wirelessly interface with a warehouse management system, which acts as an end-system computer device.

Users can adapt many existing computer devices to operate on a wireless network. A user, for example, can purchase and install a wireless network interface card (NIC) within his laptop to enable operation on a particular type of wireless network. Some devices, such as a wireless bar code scanner, operate only on a wireless network.

A computer device also has an operating system, such as Windows XP, LINUX, or MAC OS. The operating system runs software needed to realize the wireless network application. In some cases, the operating system has built-in features that enhance wireless networks. For example, Windows XP has the ability to automatically identify and associate with wireless LANs.

NICs

The *network interface card* provides the interface between the computer device and the wireless network infrastructure. The NIC fits inside the computer device, but external network adaptors are available that plug in and remain outside the computer device. Figure 2-3 shows examples of several types of wireless NICs.

Figure 2-3   Wireless NICs Have Various Types of Form Factors

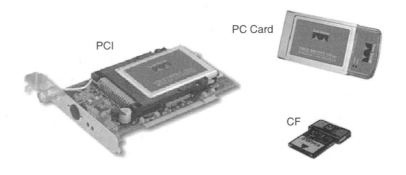

Wireless network standards define how a wireless NIC operates. For example, a wireless LAN NIC might implement the IEEE 802.11b standard. In this case, the wireless NIC will only be able to interface with a wireless network infrastructure that complies with the 802.11b standard. As a result, users must be careful to ensure that the wireless NIC they choose matches the type of wireless network infrastructure they want to access.

Wireless NICs also comply with a specific form factor, which defines the physical and electrical bus interface that enables the card to communicate with the computer device. Again, the user must consider this to ensure that the chosen wireless NIC will fit within their computer device. The following is a summary of the different internal form factors available for wireless networks:

- **Industry-Standard Architecture (ISA)**—ISA has been around since the early 1980s. Because of this, the proliferation of the ISA bus has been significant. Despite its limited performance, nearly all PCs manufactured up until recently had at least one ISA bus. The ISA bus has failed, however, to advance at the pace of the rest of the computer world, and other higher-speed alternatives are now available. ISA doesn't impose too much of a performance impact on 802.11b wireless LANs. It's not advisable, however, to purchase new ISA cards because of the possibility of them becoming obsolete.

- **Peripheral Component Interconnect (PCI)**—The PCI bus is the most popular interface for PCs today and boasts high performance. Intel originally developed and released PCI in 1993, and it satisfies the needs of the recent generations of PCs for multimedia and graphics. PCI cards were the first to popularize "plug-and-play" technology, which makes it easy to install the NIC. PCI circuitry can recognize compatible PCI cards and work with the computer's operating system to set the configurations for each card. This saves time and prevents installation headaches for nontechnical users.

- **PC Card**—The PC Card was developed in the early 1990s by the Personal Computer Memory Card International Association (PCMCIA). The *PC Card* is a credit-card-sized device that provides extended memory, modems, connectivity to external devices, as well as wireless LAN capabilities to small computer devices such as laptops and PDAs. In fact, they are the most widely available NICs available. They are more popular than ISA or PCI cards because of use in a growing number of laptops and PDAs.

It's possible to share a PC Card with a desktop PC by using an adaptor that converts a PC Card into a PCI card. This allows purchasing one NIC for use in both types of computers. You can take the PC Card with you on a business trip— or home from work— and utilize the same card when back in the office using a PC. Some PDAs require a sled device that accommodates the PC Card and mounts underneath the PDA. This is the only way to add wireless network capability to some older PDAs. The combination of the sled, PC Card and PDA, however, adds a lot of bulk and weight that depletes the usability.

- **Mini-PCI**— A Mini-PCI card is a smaller version of a standard desktop PCI card and fits well within small, mobile computer devices. It has all the same features and functionality of a normal PCI card, but is about one quarter the size. Mini-PCI cards are integrated within laptops as an option to buyers. A strong advantage of this form of radio NIC is that it frees up the PC Card slot for other devices, such as memory extenders and graphics accelerators. In addition, manufacturers can provide Mini-PCI–based wireless NICs at lower costs. The Mini-PCI card is not without disadvantages, however. The replacement of a Mini-PCI card typically requires the disassembly of the laptop, which might void the manufacturer's warranty. Mini-PCI cards might also lead to lower performance because they require the computer to do some, if not all, of the processing. Despite these drawbacks, the Mini-PCI card is becoming a solid technology in the wireless laptop world.

- **CompactFlash**— SanDisk Corporation first introduced *CompactFlash (CF)* in 1994, but wireless NICs were not available in CF form factors until recently. A CF card is small, weighing half an ounce, and is less than half the thickness of a PC Card. It also holds only one quarter the volume of PC Card radio card. The CF cards draw little power, which enables the batteries to last longer than devices using PC Cards. Some PDAs come with direct CF interfaces, which results in a lightweight and compact wireless PDA. If the computer device doesn't have a CF slot, you can purchase an adapter so that the CF card will fit into a standard PC Card slot. A CF radio card is definitely the way to go, especially for compact computing devices.

In addition to the internal NICs, a variety of external network interfaces connect to the computer device through parallel, serial, and USB ports. These might be suitable for stationary computers, but they certainly hinder mobility in most wireless applications.

As Chapter 3, "Radio Frequency and Light Signal Fundamentals: The Invisible Medium," discusses in detail, a wireless NIC includes an antenna that converts electrical signals to radio or light waves for propagation through the air medium. Antennae employ many structures, and they can be external, internal, permanent, or detachable. The antenna for a PC Card, for example, generally attaches to the end of the card and protrudes out the side of the laptop.

Mini-PCI cards, however, might have an antenna that resides inside the outer edge of a laptop monitor. Some NICs have antennaes that are permanent, which have one particular propagation pattern. Other NICs allow the replacement of the antenna, which increases flexibility in choosing an antenna that best satisfies requirements.

Air Medium

Air serves many purposes, such as providing a basis for speech, enabling air travel, and sustaining life. Air also provides a medium for the propagation of wireless communications signals, which is the heart of wireless networking. Air is the conduit by which information flows between computer devices and the wireless infrastructure. Think of communication through a wireless network as similar to talking to someone. As you move farther apart, it's more difficult to hear each other, especially when a loud noise is present.

Wireless information signals also travel through the air, but they have special properties that enable propagation over relatively long distances. Wireless information signals cannot be heard by humans, so it's possible to amplify the signals to a higher level without disturbing human ears. The quality of transmission, however, depends on obstructions in the air that either lessen or scatter the strength and range of the signals.

Rain, snow, smog, and smoke are examples of elements that impair propagation of wireless communications signals. In fact, a heavy downpour of rain can limit signal range by 50 percent while the rain is occurring. Other obstacles, such as trees and buildings, can impact the propagation and performance of the wireless network. These issues become most important when planning the installation of a wireless MAN or WAN.

With wireless networks, the air medium supports the propagation of radio and light waves that travel from one point to another. These types of signals have been in use for more than 100 years, but they are still somewhat mysterious and not well understood by most computer professionals. Chapter 3 provides details on signal characteristics and impairments that relate to the air medium.

Wireless Network Infrastructures

The infrastructure of a wireless network interconnects wireless users and end systems. The infrastructure might consist of *base stations*, access controllers, application connectivity software, and a distribution system. These components enhance wireless communications and fulfill important functions necessary for specific applications.

Base Stations

The base station is a common infrastructure component that interfaces the wireless communications signals traveling through the air medium to a wired network—often referred to as a distribution system. Therefore, a base station enables users to access a wide range of network services, such as web browsing, e-mail access, and database applications. A base station often contains a wireless NIC that implements the same technology in operation by the user's wireless NIC.

Base stations go by different names, depending on their purpose. An *access point*, for instance, represents a generic base station for a wireless LAN. A collection of access points within a wireless LAN, for example, supports roaming throughout a facility. The NIC within a user's computer device connects with the nearest access point, which provides an interface with systems within the infrastructure and users associated with other access points. As the user moves to a part of the facility that's closer to another access point, the NIC automatically reconnects with the closest access point to maintain reliable communications.

Residential gateways and routers are more advanced forms of base stations that enable additional network functions. The gateway might have functions, such as access control and application connectivity, that better serve distributed, public networks. On the other hand, a *router* would enable operation of multiple computers on a single broadband connection.

As show in Figure 2-4, a base station might support point-to-point or point-to-multipoint communications. Point-to-point systems enable communications signals to flow from one particular base station or computer device directly to another one. This is a common infrastructure for supporting long-range wireless communications links. For example, a *wireless Internet service provider (WISP)* can use this system to transport communications signals from a base station at a remote site— such as a home or office— to a base station near a communications facility.

Figure 2-4   Base Stations Support Different Configurations

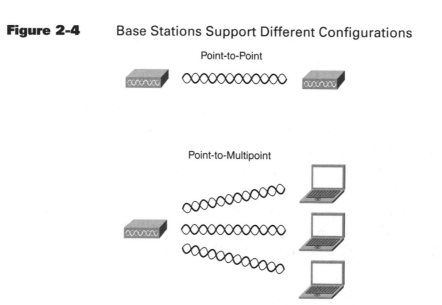

As the name implies, point-to-multipoint functionality enables a base station to communicate with more than one wireless computer device or base station. An access point within a wireless LAN implements this form of communications. The access point represents a single point whereby many computer devices connect to and communicate with each other and systems within the wireless infrastructure.

Access Controllers

In the absence of adequate security, quality of service (QoS), and roaming mechanisms in wireless network standards, companies offer access-control solutions to strengthen wireless systems. The key component to these solutions is an access controller, which is typically hardware that resides on the wired portion of the network between the access points and the protected side of the network. Access controllers provide centralized intelligence behind the access points to regulate traffic between the open wireless network and important resources. In some cases, the access point contains the access control function.

Access controllers apply to a wide range of applications. In a public wireless LAN, for example, an access controller regulates access to the Internet by authenticating and authorizing users based on a subscription plan. Similarly, a corporation can implement an access controller to help a hacker sitting in the company's parking lot from getting entry to sensitive data and applications.

The use of an access controller reduces the need for smart access points, which are relatively expensive and include many non-802.11 features. Generally, vendors refer to these smarter access points as being enterprise-grade components. Proponents of access controllers, however, argue that 802.11 access points should focus on RF excellence and low cost. Proponents also argue that access points should centralize access control functions in an access controller that serves all access points. These thin access points primarily implement the basic wireless network standard (such as IEEE 802.11), and not much more.

The users of access controllers realize the following benefits when deployed with thin access points:

- **Lower Costs**—Access points with limited functionality cost less, which generally results in lower overall system costs. This is especially true for networks requiring a larger number of access points, such as an enterprise system. The use of thin access points results in cost savings of approximately $400 per acccss point. In larger networks, this savings far outwcighs the additional cost of an access controller, which costs $5000 on the average.

- **Open Connectivity**—Smart access points offer enhancements related to security and performance to the basic wireless connectivity that wireless network standards offer. The problem in many cases is that these enhancements are only possible if the user devices implement a wireless NIC made by the same vendor as the access point. This significantly reduces the openness of the system and limits the selection of vendors. On the other hand, thin access points can easily communicate using the basic wireless network *protocol* with wireless NICs made by multiple vendors, while the access controller transparently provides enhancements.

- **Centralized Support**—An advantage of placing the smarts of the network in an access controller is that the system is easier to support, primarily because fewer touch points are in the network. If all of the intelligence of the network is within the access points, support personnel must interface with many points when configuring, monitoring, and troubleshooting the network. An access controller enables the access points to have fewer functions, reducing the need to interface with the access points when performing support tasks.

Access controllers often provide port-based access control, allowing administrators to configure access to specific applications on a per-user basis. The port, which is actually a number (such as 80 for http), corresponds to a specific type of application. For example, an access controller can block access to port 80, which forces a user to log in before being able to browse web pages. After users enter their username and password, the access controller will validate their identity through an authentication server. The network application could, as an alternative, use *digital certificates* for authentication purposes. This function regulates the user access to the protected network.

Access controllers generally employ the following features:

- **Authentication**—Most access controllers have a built-in database for authenticating users; however, some offer external interfaces to authentication servers such as *Remote Authentication Dial-In User Service (RADIUS)* and *Lightweight Directory Access Protocol (LDAP)*. For smaller, private networks, an internal database might suffice. For enterprise solutions, however, external and centralized authentication servers provide better results.

- **Encryption**—Some access controllers provide encryption of data from the client to the server and back, using such common methods such as *IPSec*. This provides added protection beyond what the native wireless network standard provides. Some of these features, however, are also part of web browsers.

- **Subnet Roaming**—In order to support roaming from one network to another, access controllers provide roaming across *subnets* without needing to re-authenticate with the system. As a result, users can continue utilizing their network applications without interruption as they roam about a facility. This feature is especially useful for larger installations where access to the network for specific users will span multiple subnets.

- **Bandwidth Management**—Because users share bandwidth in a wireless network, it's important to have a mechanism to ensure specific users don't hog the bandwidth. Access controllers provide this form of bandwidth management through the assignment of user profiles based on required QoS levels. A profile specifies the types of services, such as web browsing, e-mail, and video streaming, as well as performance limits. For example, an unsubscribed visitor attempting to utilize a public wireless LAN could classify as fitting a "visitor" profile, which might only allow access to information related to the local hotspot. A subscriber, however, could have a different role that allows him to have a broadband Internet connection.

Application Connectivity Software

Web surfing and e-mail generally perform well over wireless networks. All it takes is a browser and e-mail software on the *client device*. Users might lose a wireless connection from time to time, but the protocols in use for these relatively simple applications are resilient under most conditions.

Beyond these simple applications, however, special application connectivity software is necessary as an interface between a user's computer device and the end system hosting the application's software or database. Applications could be warehouse management software running on an IBM AS/400, a modeling application located on a UNIX box, or a time-management system residing on an old mainframe system. The databases are part of a client/server system where part, or all of the application software, resides on the client device and interfaces with a database such as Oracle or Sybase. In these cases, application connectivity software is important in addition to access points and controllers to enable communications between the user's computer device and the application software or databases located on a centralized server.

The following are various types of application connectivity software:

- **Terminal Emulation**—Terminal emulation software runs on a computer device, making the device operate as a terminal that provides a relatively simple user interface to application software running on another computer. The terminal merely presents screens to the user and accepts input rendered by the applications software. For example, VT220 *terminal emulation* communicates with applications running on a UNIX host, 5250 terminal emulation works with IBM AS/400-based systems, and 3270 terminal emulation interfaces with IBM mainframes.

  The advantage of using terminal emulation is its low initial cost and changes made to the application automatically take affect when the user logs in. Wireless systems using terminal emulation, however, might not be able to maintain continuous connections with legacy applications, which have timeouts set for more reliable wired networks. Timeouts will automatically disconnect a session if they don't sense activity within a given time period. As a result, IT groups might spend a lot of time responding to end-user complaints of dropped connections and incomplete data transactions. Therefore, implementing terminal emulation can have a disastrous effect on long-term support costs.

- **Direct Database Connectivity**—Direct database connectivity, sometimes referred to as client/server, encompasses application software running on the user's computer device. With this configuration, the software on the end-user device provides all application functionality and generally interfaces to a database located on a central server. This enables flexibility when developing applications because the programmer has complete control over what functions are implemented—and is not constrained by a legacy application located on a central computer. Direct database connections are often the best approach when needing flexibility in writing the application software. A problem, however, is that the direct database approach depends on the use of Transmission Control Protocol/Internet Protocol (TCP/IP), which is not well-suited for communications across a wireless network.

- **Wireless Middleware**—Wireless middleware software provides intermediate communications between user computer devices and the application software or database located on a server. (See Figure 2-5.) The middleware—which runs on a dedicated computer (middleware gateway) attached to the wired network—processes the packets that pass between the user computer devices and the servers. The middleware software primarily offers efficient and reliable communications over the wireless network while maintaining appropriate connections to application software and databases on the server through the more reliable wired network. Sometimes this is referred to as session persistence.

Figure 2-5   Wireless Middleware Efficiently Interconnects Computer Device Applications to Hosts and Servers

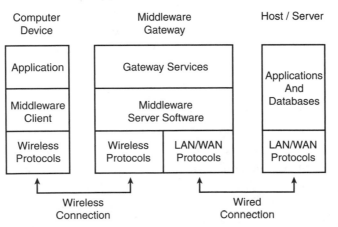

Look for the following features in middleware products:

— **Optimization techniques**—Many middleware products include data compression to help reduce the number of packets sent over the wireless link. Some implementations of middleware use proprietary communications protocols, which have little overhead as compared to traditional protocols, such as TCP/IP.

— **Intelligent restarts**—With wireless networks, a transmission can be unexpectedly cut at midstream. Intelligent restart is a recovery mechanism that detects the premature end of a transmission. When the connection is reestablished, the middleware resumes transmission from the break point instead of at the beginning. This avoids errors from occurring in applications that utilize databases.

— **Data bundling**—Some middleware is capable of combining smaller data packets into a single large packet for transmission over the wireless network, which can help lower transmission service costs of WANs. Since some wireless data services charge users by the packet, data bundling results in a lower aggregate cost.

— **Screen scraping and reshaping**—The development environment of some middleware products allows developers to use visual tools to shape and reshape portions of existing application screens to more effectively fit data on the smaller display of some non-PC wireless devices, such as PDAs and bar code scanners.

— **End system support**—Wireless middleware interfaces with a variety of end system applications and databases. If clients need access to tomultiple types of applications and databases, wireless middleware acts as a concentrator. For example, a user can use the middleware connection to interface with applications on an AS/400 and UNIX box simultaneously without needing to be concerned about running the correct terminal emulation software.

Distribution System

A wireless network is seldom entirely free of wires. The distribution system, which often includes wiring, is generally necessary to tie together the access points, access controllers, and servers. In most cases, the common Ethernet comprises the distribution system.

The IEEE *802.3* standard is the basis for Ethernet and specifies the use of the carrier sense multiple access (CSMA) protocol to provide access to a shared medium, such as twisted-pair wiring, coaxial cable, and optical fiber. CSMA is the predominant medium access standard in use today by both wired and wireless networks.

CSMA enables sharing of a common medium by allowing only one NIC to transmit information at any particular time. This is similar to a meeting environment where people (like NICs) speak only when no one else is talking. This gives each person responsibility in a way that distributes speaking decisions to each person. If more than one person talks at the same time, a collision occurs, and each person needs to take turns repeating what he said.

All computer devices on the network must take turns using the medium with Ethernet hubs. An Ethernet switch, however, enables multiple collision domains that can allow simultaneous transmission among users to improve performance. For larger networks beyond the size of a home or small office application, be sure to use switches for optimum performance.

Ethernet employs twisted-pair wiring, coaxial cable, and optical fiber for interconnecting network devices, such as access points and other distribution equipment. The use of coaxial cables in older wired LANs was common 10 years ago, but today most companies use twisted-pair wiring and optical fiber. The Electronic Industries Association (EIA) and Telecommunications Industry Association (TIA) specifies Category 5 (referred to as Cat 5) twisted-pair wiring, the most popular of all twisted-pair cables in use today with Ethernet.

Cat 5 consists of four unshielded twisted pairs of 24-gauge wires that support Ethernet signals over 100 meters (m)— about 300 feet— of cabling. Ethernet repeaters increase this range if necessary, which is one method of reaching a wireless network base station that's beyond 100 m from a communications closet.

There are also other variations of twisted-pair wiring. Enhanced Cat 5 (referred to as Cat5e) makes use of all four pairs of wires to support short-range Gigabit Ethernet (1000 Mbps) connectivity. It is also backward compatible with regular Cat 5. Cat 6 and Cat 7 cable are now available, bringing more bandwidth and range to copper-based Gigabit Ethernet networks. Cat 7 cable features individually shielded twisted pairs (STP) of wires, making it ideal for installation in locations where there is a high potential for electromagnetic interference.

The following are specific types of twisted-pair options for Ethernet common to wireless LAN distribution systems:

- **10BASE-T**—10BASE-T is one of the 802.3 physical layers and specifies data rates of 10 Mbps. A typical 10BASE-T cable uses two of the four pairs within a Cat 5 cable for sending and receiving data. Each end of the cable includes RJ-45 connectors that are a little larger than the common RJ-11 telephone connector used within North America.

  The advantage of having extra pairs of wires open is support for other uses, such as Power-over-Ethernet (PoE). This is a mechanism in which a module injects DC current into the Cat 5 cable, enabling you to supply power to the access point from the communications closet. PoE often eliminates the need for having an electrician install new electrical outlets at every access point. For larger networks, definitely consider the use of PoE.

- **100BASE-T**—Another 802.3 physical layer, 100BASE-T supports data rates of 100 Mbps. Similar to 10BASE-T Ethernet, 100-Base-T uses twisted-pair wiring, with the following options:

  - 100BASE-TX uses two pairs of Cat 5 twisted-pair wires.

  - 100BASE-T4 uses four pairs of older, lower-quality (Cat 3) twisted-pair wires.

Most implementations today use 100BASE-TX cabling. As with 10BASE-T, PoE can make use of unused pairs of wires. 100-Base-T4 was popular when needing to support 100-Mbps data rates over the older Cat 3 cabling, which was prominent during the early 1990s.

■ **Optical Fiber**—Optical fiber is more expensive than twisted pair, but fiber can be cost effective because it supports gigabit speeds and has a range of up to two kilometers. Instead of using the traditional electrical-signal-over-copper-wire approach, optical fiber cable uses pulses of light over tiny strips of glass or plastic. This makes optical fiber cable resistant to electromagnetic interference, making it valuable in situations where electronic emissions are a concern. In addition, it's nearly impossible to passively monitor the transmission of data through optical fiber cable, making it more secure than twisted-pair wiring.

With wireless LANs, optical fiber is a possible solution for reaching an access point located beyond a 100 m from a communications closet. This requires the use of an expensive pair of transceivers, however, which transforms electrical signals into light (and vice versa). One issue when dealing with optical fiber cable is the difficulties in splicing cables. You must work with glass or plastic materials that require precise alignment. You need special tools and training to make effective optical fiber cables. You should purchase precut fiber cables to avoid problems that are difficult to troubleshoot.

Management Systems

As with other types of networks, enterprise wireless networks require effective management that ensures user needs are met over the life of the network. A network management system, which involves both people and software tools, satisfies this need. The following are functions that management systems should provide.

Security

The security element involves mechanisms that avoid the compromise or damage of network resources, such as databases and e-mail messages. This includes enforcing security policies for the configuration of the wireless network in a way that counters issues related to the propagation of wireless signals. For example, policies could specify the use of a particular type of encryption to ensure a mischievous person can't receive and decode e-mail messages being sent between a user and an access point.

For more details on wireless network security methods, refer to Chapter 8, "Wireless Network Security: Protecting Information Resources."

Help Desk

The help desk provides the first level of support for users. A user having difficulties with a wireless connection should know how to reach the help desk. Users often have problems with association or experience erratic performance.

Help desk personnel are capable of solving simple connection problems, such as assisting the user configure a radio card and operating system to comply with specific wireless network policies. The help desk should have a communications interface with more advanced support functions, such as maintenance and engineering, to solve more complex problems that arise from contact with users.

Configuration Management

Configuration management consists of controlling changes made to the wireless network architecture and installed system. Changes might consist of installing or moving access points, changing access point parameters, and updating firmware. Because of the dynamic nature of wireless networks, changes are more common than with wired networks.

An enterprise should review all wireless network modification proposals that impact the performance or security of the network. This review enables a company to take into account relevant implications that involve additional costs and use of resources. The company should implement an independent design review process that evaluates each proposed wireless network solution and verifies conformance to a common architecture and support elements. The verification should, for example, include reviewing access point placement, radio frequency channel assignments, and security settings.

Network Monitoring

Network monitoring includes continuously measuring various attributes of the wireless network, including access point utilization and user traffic routes through the distribution system. This plays a key role in proactively managing the wireless network to support a growth of users and solve issues before they hamper the performance and security of the network.

An enterprise should continually measure the usage of base stations to properly scale the wireless network as user traffic changes. Base stations act as a gauge to indicate when additional base stations, access controllers, and Internet bandwidth are necessary. A problem with wireless networks is that network managers might not notice that a base station is inoperative for quite some time.

In most cases, coverage from base stations overlaps, and users will likely associate with another base station at lower performance if the primary access point is not available. Network monitoring tools, however, will notice the outage immediately and alert the appropriate support person. If possible, a company should integrate the wireless network monitoring function with tools already in use in the existing corporate network. This simplifies operational support.

Reporting

The reporting element offers information regarding various aspects of the wireless network, including usage statistics, security alarm notifications, and performance. These reports are necessary for managers to effectively gauge the operation of the network and make decisions on changes. This reporting should, at a minimum, indicate potential breaches of security, inoperable access points, and utilization. This type of information should be available to all operational support functions, such as the help desk, maintenance, and engineering.

Engineering

The engineering element provides advanced technical support for reengineering the wireless network to include newer technologies and solve problems to ensure effective performance and security. Ordinarily, the company or group that designs the initial wireless network will perform the engineering functions. The engineering function should review and verify compliance of designs with the common architectural design. In addition, the engineering group should continually monitor the evolution of wireless network technologies and products to ensure effective migration in a manner that meets growing network utilization.

Maintenance

The maintenance element repairs and configures the wireless network, including replacing broken antennae, setting channels on access points, and re-evaluating radio wave propagation. Some maintenance tasks might result from the engineering support function. For example, engineers might find the need to install an additional access point in an area where new coverage is necessary. In this case, maintenance personnel would install the access point at a location that the engineer identifies.

An important task for maintaining the wireless network is to periodically upgrade the firmware in access points. This ensures that the access point operates with the latest features and freedom from defects, which maximizes performance and security. As a result, a company should institute regular upgrades to firmware as new versions become available.

The maintenance group should also periodically perform coverage tests to ensure that the access points are properly covering the facilities at applicable levels of performance. This is necessary as the company modifies the structure of the facilities, which changes the radio wave propagation characteristics. If discrepancies are found, the maintenance group should report findings to the engineering group for resolution.

Network Architecture

The architecture of a network defines the protocols and components necessary to satisfy application requirements. One popular standard for illustrating the architecture is the seven-layer Open System Interconnect (OSI) Reference Model, developed by the International Standards Organization (ISO). OSI specifies a complete set of network functions, grouped into layers (see Figure 2-6), which reside within each network component. The OSI Reference Model is also a handy model for representing the various standards and interoperability of a wireless network.

Figure 2-6   Layers of the OSI Reference Model Represent All Functions of a Network

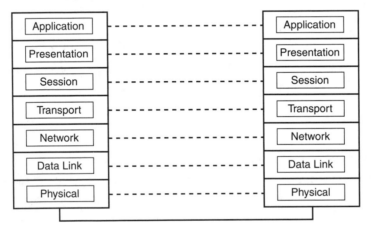

The OSI layers provide the following network functionality:

■ **Layer 7—Application layer:** Establishes communications among users and provides basic communications services such as file transfer and e-mail. Examples of software that runs at this layer include Simple Mail Transfer Protocol (SMTP), HyperText Transfer Protocol (HTTP) and File Transfer Protocol (FTP).

■ **Layer 6—Presentation layer:** Negotiates data transfer syntax for the application layer and performs translations between different data formats, if necessary. For example, this layer can translate the coding that represents the data when communicating with a remote system made by a different vendor.

- **Layer 5—Session layer:** Establishes, manages, and terminates sessions between applications. Wireless middleware and access controllers provide this form of connectivity over wireless networks. If the wireless network encounters interference, the session layer functions will suspend communications until the interference goes away.

- **Layer 4—Transport layer:** Provides mechanisms for the establishment, maintenance, and orderly termination of virtual circuits, while shielding the higher layers from the network implementation details. In general, these circuits are connections made between network applications from one end of the communications circuit to another (such as between the web browser on a laptop to a web page on a server). Protocols such as *Transmission Control Protocol (TCP)* operate at this layer.

- **Layer 3—Network layer:** Provides the routing of packets though a network from source to destination. This routing ensures that data packets are sent in a direction that leads to a particular destination. Protocols such as Internet Protocol (IP) operate at this layer.

- **Layer 2—Data link layer:** Ensures medium access, as well as synchronization and error control between two entities. With wireless networks, this often involves coordination of access to the common air medium and recovery from errors that might occur in the data as it propagates from source to destination. Most wireless network types have a common method of performing data link layer functions independent of the actual means of transmission.

- **Layer 1—Physical layer:** Provides the actual transmission of information through the medium. Physical layers include radio waves and infrared light.

The combined layers of a network architecture define the functionality of a wireless network, but wireless networks directly implement only the lower layers of the model. A wireless NIC, for example, implements the data link layer and physical layer functions. Other elements of the network (such as wireless middleware), however, offer functions that the session layer implements. In some cases, the addition of a wireless network might impact only the lower layers, but attention to higher layers is necessary to ensure that applications operate effectively in the presence of wireless network impairments.

Each layer of the OSI model supports the layers above it. In fact, the lower layers often appear transparent to the layers above. For example, TCP operating at the transport layer establishes connections with applications at a distant host computer, without awareness that lower layers are taking care of synchronization and signaling.

As shown in Figure 2-6, protocols at each layer communicate across the network to the respective peer layer. The actual transmission of data, however, occurs at the physical layer. As a result, the architecture allows for a layering process where a particular layer embeds its protocol information into frames that are placed within frames at lower layers. The frame that is sent by the physical layer actually contains frames from all higher layers. At the destination, each layer passes applicable frames to higher layers to facilitate the protocol between peer layers.

Information Signals

Data is a type of information that the network stores in a computer or retrieves from it. As a result, wireless networks transfer data from one computer to another. This data can include e-mail messages, files, web pages, video, music, and voice conversations.

Communications systems—such as a wireless network— symbolize data using codes that electrical, radio, and light signals efficiently represent. The signals carry the information through the system from one point to another. The signals are either digital or analog, depending on their location within the system.

Digital Signals

Digital signals, which are found inside computers, vary in amplitude steps as time advances. (See Figure 2-7.) Digital signals are usually binary (two-state); therefore, it is common to refer to the signal as a string of binary digits (bits) or binary data. Digital circuitry inside the computer easily stores and processes these digital signals in binary form.

Figure 2-7   Digital Signals Are Ideal for Use in Computers

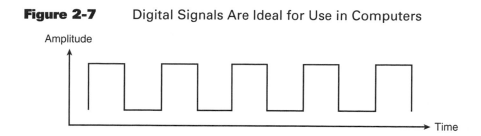

Binary is a system that only uses 0s and 1s to represent the numbers. Conversions are easy from the more familiar decimal numbering system to binary, and computers can readily store binary numbers. With some protocols, the binary values within a data frame represent specific protocol information.

One of the advantages of digital signals is easy signal regeneration. As a signal propagates through the air medium, it might encounter noise or interference that changes the appearance of the signal's waveform. To clean up and regenerate the signal, digital circuitry can detect if a digital pulse is present at a certain period of time and create a new pulse that is exactly equal to the one originally sent. As a result, a digital signal can be sent over vast distances through periodic repeaters while preserving the integrity of the information. This is not possible with analog signals.

For security purposes, it is often necessary to encrypt and later decode a signal at the destination. This process is simple with digital signals because all that is necessary is to rearrange the bits using some type of secret keying process. When the destination receives the data, a device can use the same key and decrypt the data.

The following defines important characteristics of digital signals:

- **Data rate**—The data rate corresponds to the speed that a digital signal transfers data across a wireless network. As a result, the data rate of a digital signal gives some insight on how long it will take to send data from one point to another, as well as identify the amount of **bandwidth** that the medium must supply to effectively support the signal.

The data rate of a signal is equal to the total number of bits transmitted in relation to the time it takes to send them. The common unit of measure for bit rate is bits per second (bps). As an example, consider a signal that moves 1,000,000 bits in 1 second. The data rate is 1,000,000/1 = 1,000,000 bps (or 1 Mbps).

■ **Throughput**—Throughput is similar to data rate; however, throughput calculations generally exclude the bits that correspond to the overhead that communications protocols include. There are no standards for representing throughput, but it usually includes only the actual information being sent across the network. As a result, throughput gives a more accurate way of representing the true performance and efficiency of a network. This makes throughput important when comparing wireless networks because it's directly related to performance. The higher the throughput, the higher the performance.

The data rate of a wireless LAN, for example, might be 11 Mbps, but the throughput might be only 5 Mbps. After removing the overhead—frame headers, error checking fields, acknowledgement frames, and retransmissions because of errors—the resulting information transfer is considerably lower. As the number of users increases, contention for the shared medium increases, which drives throughput even lower because computer devices (wireless NICs, to be more precise) must wait longer before sending data. This delay, which is a form of overhead, can significantly lower the throughput.

With wireless networks, it is common to say that the system sends data bits. In reality, a wireless network converts the binary digital signals into analog before transmitting the signal through the air medium.

Analog Signals

An *analog signal*, shown in Figure 2-8, is one where the amplitude of the signal varies continuously as time progresses. Much of the natural environment produces signals that are analog in form. Examples of this are light and the human voice. Man-made signals, such as radio waves, are also analog in form.

Figure 2-8   Analog Signals Carry Information Through the Air Medium

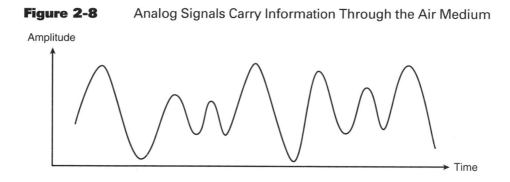

In the early days of electronic communication, most systems processed signals in analog form, mainly because their inputs were information coming from humans. An analog signal has amplitude, in units of voltage or power, and a frequency (having a specific number of cycles per second often referred to as *Hertz*). Wireless networks generally use analog signals at 2.4 GHz, which is in a band of frequencies referred to as radio waves. There are several different methods for describing the amplitude of wireless signals. Refer to Chapter 3 for details on wireless analog signals.

Flow of Information Through a Wireless Network

Certainly the reason for having a wireless network is to support the flow of information from one point to another without wires. As information flows through the network, the information changes form to efficiently traverse the network. Specific functions related to the transfer of information, such as medium access and error control, are common across the various types of wireless networks.

End Points of Information Flow

The flow of information often begins and ends with users. A business person might send an e-mail message from an airport, a doctor might review a patient's medical record from a wireless PDA, or a warehouse clerk might enter the number of items in a bin as part of inventory management. When users communicate information, they might use text, images, voice, or video through a computer device.

Initially, this information might simply be thoughts within a person's brain, which the user enters into a form of information, such as text or voice, and which the computer device stores as data. In the case of human users, the information is generally in an analog form; the information might be a digital signal when going between a nonhuman user, such as a robot, and a computer device.

Inputting, Storing, and Displaying Information

Information flows from the user to a computer device, which enables the inputting of information through a keyboard, keypad, microphone, or video camera. Newer input methods also allow information input through eye movements and brain waves. Analog signals represent the information.

Before the computer device is capable of storing the information, however, the system must convert analog information signals into a digital form that is suitable for the computer device. Analog-to-digital (A/D) converters make this possible. Special circuitry samples the analog signal, resulting in pulses with amplitudes that binary numbers can represent. Likewise, digital-to-analog (D/A) converters translate digital signals into analog ones as part of presenting the information to users.

Inside a computer device, special codes represent information as data. The American Standard Code for Information Interchange (ASCII) code, for example, represents English characters as numbers. A computer stores these numbers as data. As examples, the ASCII code (in hexadecimal format) for the uppercase letter A is 41 and the lowercase h is 68. Most computers use ASCII encoding to represent textual information by representing the number in binary form, which includes only 1s and 0s. Other coding techniques symbolize video and audio information.

Interfacing with the Air Medium

After the user instructs the computer device to send information over the wireless network, the computer device negotiates a connection to the remote computer, which involves the use of transport and session layer functions. After establishing a connection, the computer device delivers the data in digital form to the wireless NIC. The wireless NIC generally sends a frame containing the information that conforms to a specific standard, such as IEEE 802.11, to the wireless NIC located within the remote computer device or access point.

The sending wireless NIC converts the data to an analog radio frequency or light wave signal before transmission through the antenna. This conversion requires modulation, which involves conversion of the signal from digital to analog. Chapter 3 discusses particulars on how this is done. After modulation, the signal propagates through the air medium to the receiving wireless NIC, which demodulates and processes the received signal before handing the data up to higher network architectural layers.

Medium Access

An important aspect of the transmission of data over a wireless network includes *medium access*, a data link layer function that comprises protocols that all wireless NICs must follow. These protocols ensure that wireless NICs coordinate the transmission of data, especially when only one can transmit at any particular time. Without this mechanism, several collisions would occur.

As with wired networks, CSMA is a common medium access protocol for wireless networks. CSMA implements a listen-before-talk protocol for regulating distributed access to a common medium. With CSMA, each wireless NIC has the capability of sensing transmissions from other devices.

If Node A has data to send, Node A first checks—senses—if any other nodes are transmitting data. (See Figure 2-9.) If the medium is clear—no transmission is heard—Node A will transmit one frame of data. If Node A senses transmissions from another node, Node A holds off transmitting and waits a period of time before sensing the channel again. The sensing operation continues until the node sends the data frame.

Figure 2-9   Node A Is Part of a Hypothetical Wireless Network
Where Each Node Takes Turns Transmitting Data

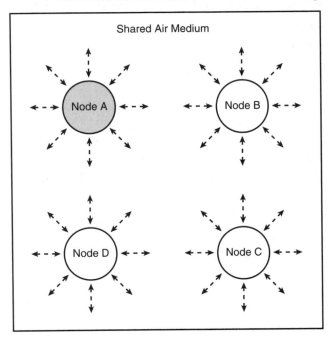

Collisions can occur with CSMA even though the transmitting node senses the channel first before sending data. The reason for this is the non-zero propagation delay between the nodes. The transmission coming from a particular node does not block all nodes from transmitting until the signal reaches all other nodes.

Node B, for example, starts to send a signal. Node A also needs to transmit a frame. It senses the medium and finds it clear because the signal from Node B has not arrived at Node A due to the propagation delay. As a result, Node A senses an idle medium and begins transmitting. Moments later, a collision between the two frames occurs, which causes significant errors in both data frames. Both nodes must retransmit the frames.

CSMA offers asynchronous access to the medium, which carries no guarantee that a particular NIC will be able to access the medium and send data within a particular span of time. Therefore, packet transmissions with CSMA are not constant.

This poses a problem for the transmission of real-time information, such as voice and video, because the network might not deliver pieces of information regularly enough to meet quality needs. In this case, QoS functions and higher throughput are necessary to improve performance.

Error Control

Information signals might encounter bit errors when propagating through the air medium. Noise and interference within the area of the wireless network causes these errors. As a result, wireless NICs implement error control mechanisms that detect and correct bit errors.

Noise from the sun's radiation and man-made devices cause damage to wireless information signals and is always present. The *noise floor*, however, is often low enough so that receivers are capable of distinguishing the information signal from the noise. At longer ranges, however, attenuation might reduce the information signal to a level that falls below the noise floor, and bit errors begin to occur.

The noise causing altered bits within wireless networks is usually Gaussian, or impulse noise. Theoretically, the amplitude of Gaussian noise is uniform across the frequency spectrum, and it normally triggers random errors that are independent of each other. Impulse noise, the most disastrous, is characterized by long quiet intervals of time followed by high-amplitude bursts. This noise results from natural causes— such as lightning— as well as man-made causes. Impulse noise is responsible for most errors in digital communication systems and generally provokes errors to occur dependently in groups. This distortion is referred to as burst errors.

Error control techniques highly reduce the number of transmission errors. Bit errors might still occur while data frames travel through the air medium, but error control mechanisms correct the errors. As a result, the transmission of information through medium appears error-free to higher-layer protocols and the users.

The two primary types of error control are automatic repeat-request (ARQ) and forward error correction (FEC). With ARQ, which operates at the data link layer, the receiving wireless NIC detects errors and uses a feedback path to the sending wireless NIC for requesting the retransmission of frames having bit errors. There are two main events that must occur to correct errors with ARQ. First, a received frame must be checked at the receiver for possible errors, and then the sender must be notified to retransmit the frames received in error. In some protocols, such as 802.11, the receiver sends an acknowledgement to the sender if the received frame has no errors. The absence of an acknowledgement indicates to the sender to retransmit the frame.

Two approaches for retransmitting unsatisfactory blocks of data exist:

- Stop-and-wait ARQ

- Continuous ARQ

Stop-and-Wait ARQ

In the stop-and-wait method of transmission, the sending NIC transmits a block of data, then stops and waits for an acknowledgment from the receiving NIC on whether a particular frame was acceptable or not. If the sending side receives a negative acknowledgment, the previous frame will be sent again. The sending NIC will send the next frame after it receives a positive acknowledgment from the receiving NIC. The IEEE 802.11 standard specifies this form of error control.

One advantage of stop-and-wait ARQ is it does not require much memory space at the sending or receiving NIC. The outstanding transmitted frame needs only to be stored at the sender (in case of retransmission). On the other hand, stop-and-wait ARQ becomes inefficient as the propagation delay between the source and desti-nation becomes large. For example, data sent on satellite links normally experi-ence a round-trip delay of several hundred milliseconds; therefore, long block lengths are necessary to maintain a reasonably effective data rate. The trouble is that with longer data blocks the probability of an error occurring in a particular block is greater. Therefore, retransmission will occur often, and the resulting throughput will be lower.

Continuous ARQ

One way of improving the throughput on longer links is to use the continuous ARQ method. With this type of ARQ, the transmitter sends data blocks continu-ously until the receiving NIC detects an error. The sending NIC is usually capable of transmitting a certain number of frames and keeps a log of which frames have been sent. Once the receiving side detects a bad block, it will send a signal back to the sending NIC requesting that the bad frame be sent over again. When the receiver gets the signal to retransmit a certain frame, several subsequent frames might have already been sent because of propagation delays between the sender and receiver.

The sending NIC can retransmit frames with continuous ARQ in several ways. One method is for the source to retrieve the erred frame from the transmit memory and send the bad frame as well as the subsequent frames. This is called the go-back-n technique, and it can be more effective than the stop-and-wait ARQ because it makes better use of the channel bandwidth. One problem though is when n—the number of frames the transmitter sent after the erred frame plus one—becomes large, the method becomes inefficient. This is because the retransmission of just one frame means that a large number of good frames will also be resent, which decreases throughput.

The go-back-n technique is useful in applications where the receiver has little memory space because all that is needed is a receiver window size of one (ability to store one frame), assuming frames do not need to be delivered in order. When the receiving NIC rejects an erred frame —sends a negative acknowledgment—it does not need to store any subsequent frames for possible reordering while it is waiting for the retransmission. It need not wait because all subsequent frames will also be resent.

An alternative to the continuous go-back-n technique is a method that selectively retransmits only the erred frame and resumes normal transmission at the point just before getting the notification of a bad block of data. This is the selective repeat approach. Selective repeat is obviously better than continuous go-back-n in terms of throughput because the sending NIC only transmits the erred data block; however, the receiver must be capable of storing a number of data frames if they are to be processed in order. The receiver needs to buffer data that have been received after an erred frame was requested for retransmission as only the damaged frame will be resent.

All ARQ types depend on the detection of errors and the retransmission of the faulty data. Overall, ARQ is best for the correction of burst errors because this type of distortion normally occurs in a small percentage of frames, and does not invoke many retransmissions. Because of the feedback inherent in ARQ protocols, *half-duplex* or *full-duplex* lines must be in use since ARQ communication occurs in both directions. If only *simplex* links are available, it is impossible to use the ARQ technique because the receiver would not be able to notify the sending NIC of bad data blocks.

As an alternative to ARQ, FEC automatically corrects as many errors as it can within the physical layer at the receiving NIC without referring to the sending NIC. This is possible because the sending NIC includes enough redundant bits in case some are lost because of errors. This makes FEC well suited for simplex communications links, and cases where a return path to the sending NIC is not feasible.

For example, consider sending data wirelessly to control a space probe orbiting Pluto. By the time the sending NIC receives a negative acknowledgement from the probe and the corresponding retransmission of data reaches the probe, the probe would likely crash because of the significant propagation delay. Most wireless networks exist on Earth, but propagation delays can still be significant enough to warrant the use of FEC.

Despite the ability of FEC to correct errors without referring to the sending NIC, ARQ is still the most common method of error control. This is mainly because errors usually occur in clusters because of impulse noise. This places a requirement to correct large numbers of errors, which FEC typically cannot accomplish without excessive amounts of redundancy.

Many communications systems, however, are utilizing a combination of both ARQ and FEC. In this case, the physical layer devices attempt to correct a small number of errors to avoid a retransmission. If FEC corrects all the errors, the ARQ mechanism will not need to resend the data frame. If there are a large number of errors, ARQ steps in and the sender will resend the frame.

Transferring Wireless Data Signals

The air medium does not offer any active components to the wireless network. Several passive elements impact the appearance and effectiveness of the wireless information signals. While propagating through the medium, for example, the signals will encounter attenuation from solid objects and weather, as well as loss because of the distance between the sending and receiving NIC. In addition, the signals propagating through the medium can encounter interference, *multipath* propagation, and other elements that can impair the signal. Refer to Chapter 3 for more details on these impairments.

Connecting with the Wireless Network Infrastructure

The base station, such as an access point, includes both a wireless and wired NIC, as well as software that interfaces the two networks. When a wireless user communicates with another wireless user, the base station might simply resend the data frame received from one user so that the other user is able to receive it. In this case, the base station is acting as a repeater. Alternatively, the base station might forward the data to the wired side of the base station if the destination is located somewhere on the wired side of the network.

Upon receiving a data frame, the wireless NIC within the base station converts the analog radio wave or light signal into a digital signal and performs error detection to ensure that the resulting data frame does not have any bit errors. The error control mechanism will cause the sending wireless NIC to retransmit the data frame if errors are present. After taking care of erred frames, the wireless NIC within the base station will either resend the frame or forward the frame to the wired side of the base station.

The wired NIC generally implements Ethernet, which interfaces directly with enterprise systems. The base station usually connects the wireless and wired networks at the physical layer and data link layer. Some base stations also include routing, which is a network layer function.

When traversing wire, the information signal remains in digital form, but different types of systems might convert the digital signal to a form suitable for transmission over the particular medium in use. The signal might undergo conversion to an analog form again if transmission over another wireless link, such as satellite, is necessary to reach the destination.

Chapter Summary

Wireless networks include components that make mobile and portable application possible. Users are end points of the wireless network and utilize computer devices designed for a particular application. Wireless NICs and base stations are key components that communicate over the air medium. To provide roaming throughout a facility or city, a distribution system such as Ethernet interconnects base stations and interfaces users to servers and applications located on the wired network.

The seven-layer OSI reference model depicts functions necessary for a network, but wireless networks implement only functions defined by the bottom two layers—the physical and data link layer. These functions include medium access, error control, and formation of radio and light signals for propagation through the medium. When deploying wireless networks, however, it's important to ensure that protocols operating at higher layers have features that counter impairments found in wireless networks.

Chapter Review Questions

You can find the answers to the following questions in Appendix A, "Answers to Chapter Review Questions."

1. Which wireless NIC form factors are best for small wireless computer devices?

2. What are examples of elements that impair the propagation of wireless communications signals through the air medium?

3. What is the primary purpose of a base station?

4. What are common features of wireless middleware?

5. On what layers of the OSI reference model do wireless networks operate?

6. How is throughput different from data rate?

7. True or false: A computer device stores data in analog form.

8. A wireless NIC must convert the information into what type of signal before transmission through the air medium?

9. Which medium access protocol is common with wireless networks?

10. Explain how the ARQ form of error control works.

What You Will Learn

After reading this chapter, you should be able to

- ✔ Understand the general attributes of radio and light signals that affect propagation through the air medium

- ✔ Understand how wireless networks transform the representation of information for transmission through the air

CHAPTER 3

Radio Frequency and Light Signal Fundamentals: The Invisible Medium

The primary difference between wireless and wired networks lies in the communications medium. Wired networks utilize cabling to transfer electrical current that represents information. With wireless networks, radio frequency (RF) and light signals have the job of carrying information invisibly through the air. This chapter continues the discussion on concepts common to all types of wireless networks, with emphasis on RF and light signal fundamentals.

Wireless Transceivers

A wireless transceiver consists of a transmitter and a receiver. In the transmitter, a process known as *modulation* converts electrical digital signals inside a computer into either RF or light, which are analog signals. Amplifiers then increase the magnitude of the signals prior to departing an *antenna*. At the destination, a receiver detects the relatively weak signals and demodulates them into data types applicable to the destination computer. These elements, which Figure 3-1 illustrate, are found in what's referred to as the transceiver. The transceiver is generally composed of hardware that is part of the wireless NIC.

Figure 3-1 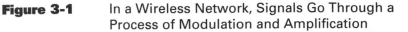 In a Wireless Network, Signals Go Through a Process of Modulation and Amplification

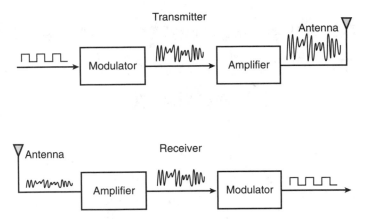

Understanding RF Signals

An *RF signal* is an electromagnetic wave that communications systems use to transport information through air from one point to another. RF signals have been in use for many years. They provide the means for carrying music to FM radios and video to televisions. In fact, RF signals are the most common means for carrying data over a wireless network.

RF Signal Attributes

The RF signal propagates between the sending and receiving stations' antennae. As shown in Figure 3-2, the signal that feeds the antenna has an amplitude, frequency, and phase. These attributes vary in time in order to represent information.

The amplitude indicates the strength of the RF signal. The measure for amplitude is generally power, which is analogous to the amount of effort a person needs to exert to ride a bicycle over a specific distance. Power, in terms of electromagnetic signals, represents the amount of energy necessary to push the signal over a particular distance. As the power increases, so does the range.

Figure 3-2   Amplitude, Frequency, and Phase Are Basic Elements of
RF Signal

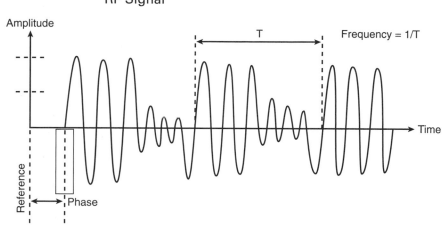

As a radio signal propagates through the air, it experiences a loss in amplitude. If
the range between the sender and receiver increases, the signal amplitude declines
exponentially. In an open environment, one clear of obstacles, the RF signals
experience what engineers call free-space loss, which is a form of attenuation.
The atmosphere causes the modulated signal to attenuate exponentially as the signal propagates farther away from the antenna. Therefore, the signal must have
enough power to reach the desired distance at a signal level acceptable that the
receiver needs.

The ability of the receiver to make sense of the signal, however, depends on the
presence of other nearby RF signals. For illustration, imagine two people, Eric
and Sierra, whom are 20 feet apart and trying to carry on a conversation. Sierra,
acting as the transmitter, is speaking just loud enough for Eric, the receiver, to
hear every word. If their baby, Madison, is crying loudly, Eric might miss a few
words. In this case, the interference of the baby has made it impossible to effectively support communications. Either Eric and Sierra need to move closer
together, or Sierra needs to speak louder. This is no different than the transmitters
and receivers in wireless systems using RF signals for communications.

The *frequency* describes how many times per second that the signal repeats itself. The unit for frequency is Hertz (Hz), which is the number of cycles occurring each second. For example, an 802.11b wireless LAN operates at a frequency of 2.4 GHz, which means that the signal includes 2,400,000,000 cycles per second.

The phase corresponds to how far the signal is offset from a reference point. As a convention, each cycle of the signal spans 360 degrees. For example, a signal might have a phase shift of 90 degrees, which means that the offset amount is one quarter (90/360 = 1/4) of the signal. A variation in phase is often useful for conveying information. For example, a signal can represent a binary 1 as a phase shift of 30 degrees and a binary 0 with a shift of 60 degrees. A strong advantage of representing data as phase shifts is that impairments resulting from the propagation of the signal through the air don't have much impact. Impairments generally affect amplitude, not the signal phase.

RF Signal Pros and Cons

As compared to using light signals, RF signals have the characteristics defined in Table 3-1.

Table 3-1 Comparing the Pros and Cons of RF Signals

RF Signal Pros	RF Signal Cons
Relatively long range, up to 20 miles when line-of-sight is possible	Lower throughput, up to the Mbps range
Good operation in haze and foggy conditions, except heavy rain causes poor performance	High potential for RF interference from other external RF-based systems
License-free operation (only for 802.11-based systems)	Limited security because of radio propagation to beyond the facilities

These pros make the use of RF signals effective for the bulk of wireless network applications. Most wireless network standards, such as 802.11 and Bluetooth, specify the use of RF signals.

RF Signal Impairments

RF signals encounter impairments, such as interference and multipath propagation. This impacts communications between the sender and receiver, often causing lower performance and unhappy users.

Interference

Interference occurs when the two signals are present at the receiving station at the same time, assuming that they have the same frequency and phase. This is similar to one person trying to listen to two others talking at the same time. In this situation, wireless NIC receivers make errors when decoding the meaning of the information being sent.

The Federal Communications Commission (FCC) regulates the use of most frequency bands and modulation types to avoid the possibility of signal interference between systems. However, radio interference can still occur, especially with systems operating in license-free bands. Users are free to install and utilize license-free equipment such as wireless LANs without coordinating usage and interference.

Figure 3-3 illustrates various forms of interference. Inward interference is where external signals interfere with the radio signal propagation of a wireless network. This interference can cause errors to occur in the information bits being sent. The receiver eventually discovers the errors, which invokes retransmissions and results in delays to the users. Significant inward interference might occur if another radio system is operating nearby with the same frequency and modulation type, such as two radio LANs operating in the license-free bands within close proximity.

Figure 3-3   Radio Signal Interference Can Be Inward or Outward

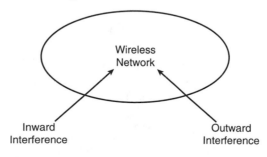

Other sources of inward interference are cordless phones, microwave ovens, and Bluetooth devices. When these types of RF devices are in use, the performance of a wireless network can significantly decrease because of retransmissions and competition on the network for use of the medium. This requires careful planning and consideration of other radio devices that might interfere with the wireless network.

One of the best ways to combat RF interference is to eliminate the sources of interference. For example, a company could set a policy for not using cordless phones that fall within the same frequency band as the wireless network. The problem, however, is that it is often impossible to completely restrict the usage of potential interferers, such as Bluetooth devices. If interference is going to be a big issue, consider choosing a wireless network that operates in a frequency band that doesn't conflict.

Outward interference happens when the signals from the radio signal system interfere with other systems. As with inward interference, significant outward interference can occur if a wireless network is in close proximity with another system. Because wireless network transmit power is relatively low, outward interference rarely causes significant problems.

Multipath

Multipath propagation occurs when portions of an RF signal take different paths when propagating from a source—such as a radio NIC—to a destination node, such as an access point. (See Figure 3-4.) A portion of the signal might go directly to the destination; and another part might bounce from a desk to the ceiling, and then to the destination. As a result, some of the signal encounters delay and travel longer paths to the receiver.

Figure 3-4   Obstacles Cause the Signal to Bounce in Different Directions

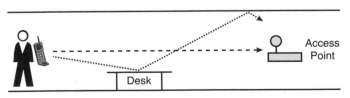

Multipath delays cause the information symbols represented in the radio signal to smear. (See Figure 3-5.) Because the shape of the signal conveys the information being transmitted, the receiver makes mistakes when demodulating the signal's information. If the delays are great enough, bit errors in the packet occur, especially when data rates are high. The receiver won't be able to distinguish the symbols and interpret the corresponding bits correctly. When multipath strikes in this way, the receiving station detects the errors through an error-checking process. In response to bit errors, the sending station eventually retransmits the data frame.

Figure 3-5   Smearing of the Signals Because of Multipath Causes Confusion and Bit Errors in Receivers

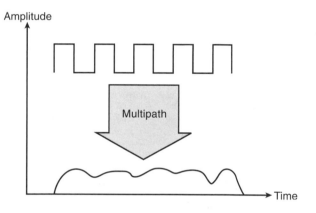

Because of retransmissions, users encounter lower performance when multipath is significant. As examples, 802.11 signals in homes and offices might encounter 50 nanoseconds (ns) multipath delay while a manufacturing plant could be as high as 300 ns. Based on these values, multipath isn't too much of a problem in homes and offices. Metal machinery and racks in a plant, however, provide a lot of reflective surfaces that cause RF signals to bounce around and take erratic paths. As a result, be wary of multipath problems in warehouses, processing plants, and other areas full of irregular, metal obstacles.

What can you do if multipath is causing problems? Aside from clearing desks and chairs from your building, diversity seems to be the best solution to combat the perils of multipath. Diversity is the use of two antennae for each radio NIC to increase the odds of receiving a better signal on either of the antennae.

Diversity antennae have physical separation from the radio to ensure that one will encounter fewer multipath propagation affects than the other. In other words, the composite signal that one antenna receives might be closer to the original than what's found at the other antenna. The receiver uses signal-filtering and decision-making software to choose the better signal for demodulation. In fact, the reverse is also true: The transmitter chooses the better antenna for transmitting in the opposite direction.

Understanding Light Signals

Light signals have been in use with communications systems for even longer than RF systems. Lanterns would provide a source of light to use with sending codes between ships at sea hundreds of years ago. Light guns are still in use today at many airports as a backup communication with aircraft having malfunctioning radio gear.

Wireless networks that utilize light signals, however, are not as common as these that use radio signals. Light signals generally satisfy needs for special applications, such as building-to-building links and short-range personal-area networks. Some wireless LANs and inter-building products use laser light to carry information between computers.

Light Signal Attributes

A light signal is analog in form and has a very high frequency that's not regulated by the FCC. Most wireless networks that use light for wireless signaling purposes utilize infrared light, which has a wavelength of approximately 900 nanometers. This equates to 333,333 GHz, which is quite a bit higher than RF signals and falls just below the visual range of humans.

Diffused and direct infrared are two main types of light transmission. Figure 3-6 illustrates these two concepts. Diffused laser light is normally reflected off a wall or ceiling, and direct laser is directly focused in a line-of-sight fashion. Most laser LANs utilize diffused infrared; inter-building modems and PDAs use the direct infrared technique.

Figure 3-6   Both Diffused and Directed Light Signals Offer a Basis for Wireless Networks

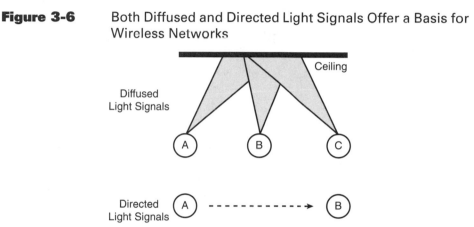

Infrared light has very high bandwidth; however, the diffusing technique severely attenuates the signal and requires slow data transmissions (less than 1 Mbps) to avoid significant transmission errors. In addition, this technique limits wireless component spacing to around 40 feet, mainly because of the lower ceilings indoors and resulting signal path geometry. The advantage is relatively easy installation with inexpensive components.

The direct infrared approach, commonly referred to as free-space optics, intensifies the light signal power similarly to a directive radio signal antenna. This increases the range of low-power laser systems to a mile or so at data rates up in the Gbps range.

As with RF signals, the amplitude of light also decreases as distance between the sending and receiving stations increase. The range of an infrared light system can vary from a few feet with PDA applications to 1 mile with direct infrared systems. This is significantly less range than with RF systems.

Light Signal Pros and Cons

As compared to RF signals, light signals have the characteristics defined in Table 3-2.

Table 3-2   Comparing the Pros and Cons of Light Signals

Light Signal Pros	Light Signal Cons
Extremely high through-put, up to the Gbps range	Variable, unreliable performance in the presence of significant smog, fog, rain, snow, and other airborne particulate matter
High inherent security because of narrow laser beam	Relatively short-range (1 mile) capability
License-free operation	Requirement for line-of-sight operation, free from obstructions such as buildings, trees, and telephone poles
Extremely low potential for RF interference from external systems	Issues dealing with alignment because of building swaying

These characteristics make the use of light signals most effective for specialized applications where extremely high performance is necessary. For example, a company can install an infrared communications link between two nearby buildings in order to facilitate high-speed server backups over a wireless network.

Light Signal Impairments

Light signal propagation is not free from difficulties. Impairments, such as interference and obstructions, limit the performance of the wireless network that uses light signals.

Interference

Light signals are free from RF sources of interference such as cordless phones, and microwave ovens. In fact, the FCC doesn't regulate light signals because of extremely limited potential interference among systems. Light signals have such a high frequency that their emissions are well outside the spectrum of RF systems, which means that the FCC doesn't regulate light signals.

Interference from other sources of light, however, can still be a problem for systems that use light signals. For example, the installation of a point-to-point infrared transmission system aimed in an easterly or westerly direction can receive substantial interference from infrared light found within sunlight because the sun is low to the horizon. This interference can be high enough in some cases to completely disrupt transmission of data on the infrared link. When installing these types of systems, be certain to follow the manufacturer's recommendations when orienting the antennae.

Attenuation Because of Obstructions and Weather

Obstructions such as buildings, mountains, and trees offer substantial amounts of attenuation to light signals as they propagate through the air. Most of these objects are composed of materials that readily absorb and scatter the light. As a result, be sure that the path between the end points of a light-based communications system are completely clear of obstacles.

Even if the communications path is open, weather can still impress large amounts of attenuation to light signals. The problem with weather is that it varies. For example, heavy fog might be present, and then the skies might be completely clear the following hour. This makes planning link budgets for light-based systems, especially those operating near the range limits, extremely difficult. Planners must be certain that the attenuation imposed by weather will not disrupt communications.

Modulation: Preparing Signals for Propagation

Modulation creates a radio or light signal from the network data so that it is suitable for propagation through the air. This involves converting the digital signal contained within the computer into an analog signal. As part of this process, modulation superimposes the information signal onto a carrier, which is a signal having a specific frequency. In effect, the information rides on top of the carrier. In order to represent the information, the modulation signal varies the carrier in a way that represents the information.

This is done because it's generally not practical to transmit the information signal in its native form. For example, consider Brian, who wants to transmit his voice wirelessly from Dayton to Cincinnati, which is about 65 miles. One approach is for Brian to use a really high-powered audio amplifier system. The problem with this is that the intense volume would probably deafen everyone in Dayton. Instead, a better approach is to modulate Brian's voice with a radio frequency or light *carrier signal* that's out of range of human hearing and suitable for propagation through the air. The information signal can vary the amplitude, frequency, or phase of the carrier signal, and amplification of the carrier will not bother humans because it's well beyond the hearing range.

The latter is precisely what modulation does. A modulator mixes the source information signal, such as voice or data, with a carrier signal. The transceiver couples the resulting modulated and amplified signals to an antenna. The modulated signal departs the antenna and propagates through the air. The receiving station antenna couples the modulated signal into a demodulator, which derives the information signal from the radio signal carrier.

One of the simplest forms of modulation is amplitude modulation, which varies the amplitude of a signal in order to represent data. This is common for light-based systems whereby the presence of a 1 data bit turns the light on, and the presence of a 0 bit turns the light off. Actual light signal codes are more complex, but the main idea is to turn the light on and off in order to send the data. This is similar to giving flashlights to people in a dark room and having them communicate with each other by flicking the flashlight on and off to send coded information.

Modulation for RF systems is more complex and covered in the following sections.

Frequency Shift-Keying

Frequency shift-keying (FSK) makes slight changes to the frequency of the carrier signal in order to represent information in a way that's suitable for propagation through the air. For example, as shown in Figure 3-7, modulation can represent a 1 or 0 data bit with either a positive or negative shift in frequency of the carrier. If the shift in frequency is negative, that is a shift of the carrier to a lower frequency; the result is a Logic 0. The receiver can detect this shift in frequency and demodulate the results as a 0 data bit.

Figure 3-7   FSK Makes Use of Changes in Frequency to
Carry Information

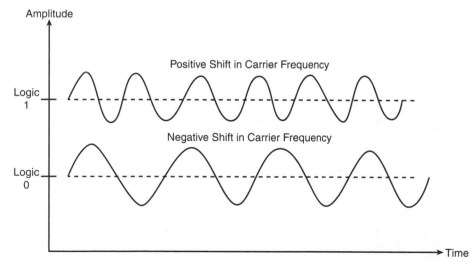

Phase Shift-Keying

Similar to FSK, some systems utilize *phase shift-keying (PSK)* for modulation purposes. With PSK, data causes changes in the signal's phase while the frequency remains constant. The phase shift, as Figure 3-8 depicts, can correspond to a specific positive or negative amount relative to a reference. A receiver is able to detect these phase shifts and realize the corresponding data bits.

Figure 3-8 PSK Makes Use of Changes in Phase to Carry Information

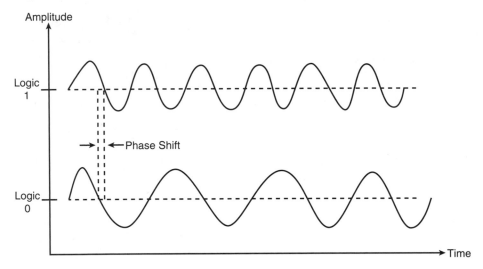

Quadrature Amplitude Modulation

Quadrature amplitude modulation (QAM) causes both the amplitude and phase of the carrier to change in order to represent patterns of data, often referred to as symbols. (See Figure 3-9.) The advantage of QAM is the capability of representing large groups of bits as a single amplitude and phase combination. In fact, some QAM-based systems make use of 64 different phase and amplitude combinations, resulting in the representation of 6 data bits per symbol. This makes it possible for standards such as 802.11a and 802.11g to support the higher data rates.

Figure 3-9   QAM Makes Use of Changes in Amplitude and Phase to Carry Information

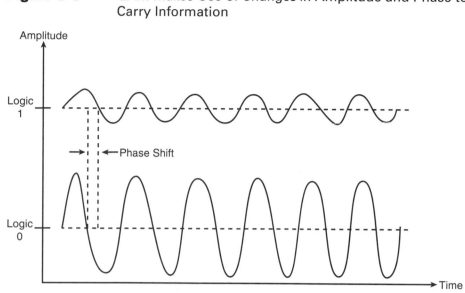

Spread Spectrum

In addition to modulating the digital signal into an analog carrier signal using FSK, PSK, or QAM, some wireless networks also spread the modulated carrier over a wider spectrum in order to comply with regulatory rules. This process, called *spread spectrum*, significantly reduces the possibility of outward and inward interference. As a result, regulatory bodies generally don't require users of spread spectrum systems to obtain licenses.

Spread spectrum, developed originally by the military, spreads a signal's power over a wide band of frequencies. (See Figure 3-10.) Spread spectrum radio components use either direct sequence or frequency hopping for spreading the signal. Direct sequence modulates a radio carrier by a digital code with a bit rate much higher than the information signal bandwidth. Frequency hopping quickly hops the radio carrier from one frequency to another within a specific range. Figures 3-11 and 3-12 illustrate direct sequence and frequency hopping, respectively.

Figure 3-10   Spread Spectrum Occupies a Wide Portion of the RF Spectrum

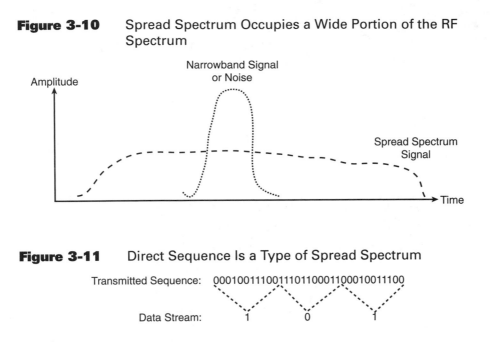

Figure 3-11   Direct Sequence Is a Type of Spread Spectrum

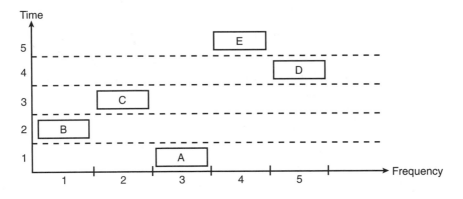

Figure 3-12   Frequency Hopping Is a Type of Spread Spectrum

Most spread spectrum systems operate within the Industrial, Scientific, and Medicine (ISM) bands, which the FCC authorized for wireless LANs in 1975. The ISM bands are located at 902 MHz, 2.400 GHz, and 5.7 GHz. RF systems operating in the ISM band must use spread spectrum modulation and operate below 1 watt transmitter output power. Commercial users who purchase ISM band products do not need to obtain or manage FCC licenses. This makes it easy to install and relocate wireless networks because the hassle of managing licenses is eliminated. Because the ISM bands are open to the public, however, care must be taken to avoid RF interference with other devices operating in the same ISM bands.

Orthogonal Frequency Division Multiplexing

Instead of using spread spectrum, some wireless systems make use of *Orthogonal Frequency Division Multiplexing (OFDM)*. OFDM divides a signal modulated with FSK, PSK, or QAM across multiple sub-carriers occupying a specific channel. (See Figure 3-13.) OFDM is extremely efficient, which enables it to provide the higher data rates and minimize multipath propagation problems.

Figure 3-13   OFDM Sends Multitudes of Data Simultaneously in Parallel

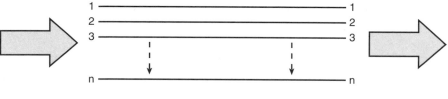

Multiple subchannels
provide parallel transmission.

OFDM is becoming popular for high-speed transmission. In addition to being part of both 802.11a and 802.11g wireless LANs, OFDM is the basis for the European-based HiperLAN/2 wireless LAN standards. In addition, OFDM has also been around for a while supporting the global standard for Asymmetric Digital Subscriber Line (ADSL), a high-speed wired telephony standard.

Ultrawideband Modulation

Ultrawideband (UWB) modulation is beginning to take a stronger foothold instead of spread spectrum or OFDM in the wireless networking industry. While it has been used for a while by the military, UWB is now going through the necessary authorizations and developments for public and commercial use. Even though the advancement of UWB has been somewhat slow, UWB becoming a superior technology for many types of wireless networks is a possibility.

UWB uses low-powered, short-pulse radio signals in order to transfer data over a wide range of frequencies. A UWB transmission involves billions of pulses spread over several gigahertz. The corresponding receiver then translates the pulses into data by listening for a familiar pulse sequence sent by the transmitter.

UWB should initially deliver bandwidths from about 40 to 600 Mbps, and eventually data rates could be up to (with higher power). UWB systems also consume little power, around one ten-thousandth of cell phones. This makes UWB practical for use in smaller devices, such as cell phones, PDAs, and even watches that users can carry at all times.

Because UWB operates at such low power, it has little interference impact on other systems. UWB causes less interference than conventional RF systems. In addition, the relatively wide spectrum that UWB utilizes significantly minimizes the impact of interference from other systems.

Concerns still remain, however, about the interference of higher-power UWB systems. The FCC plans to reevaluate UWB in the near future, and they will take a closer look at the issue of higher-power systems. Until then, you're limited to UWB products with short-range propagation.

Chapter Summary

RF and light signals are the heart of wireless networks. They offer a means of transmitting information invisibly through air. Interference offers the most critical form of transmission impairment, requiring careful planning when deploying a wireless network. The various modulation techniques—FSK, PSK, or QAM—combine with spread spectrum or OFDM to realize a transceiver, which is a critical element of the wireless NIC.

Chapter Review Questions

You can find the answers to the following questions in Appendix A, "Answers to Chapter Review Questions."

1. RF signals offer relatively short range as compared to light signals. True or false?

2. What type of weather impacts RF signals the most?

3. Why does interference cause errors in wireless networks?

4. What are sources of RF interference?

5. Multipath affects higher data rates more than lower data rates for 2.4 GHz systems. True or false?

6. What is meant by a diffused infrared light system?

7. Approximately up to what range do direct infrared systems operate?

8. How does modulation make it possible to transmit information through the air?

9. What attributes of a signal does QAM change in order to represent information?

10. Spread spectrum generally requires user licenses. True or false?

What You Will Learn

After reading this chapter, you should be able to

- ✔ Recognize specific wireless PAN applications

- ✔ Understand wireless PAN components and standards

- ✔ Realize the various wireless PAN systems

CHAPTER 4

Wireless PANs: Networks for Small Places

Wireless PANs satisfy needs for wireless networking over relatively small areas, such as between a cell phone and a laptop. In most cases, the range of a wireless PAN is less than 30 feet. This makes wireless PANs applicable to a wide variety of solutions, but many of the applications merely replace interfacing cables or allow simple transfers of information directly from one user to another.

This chapter defines each of the primary wireless PAN components, describes how these components interconnect to form a variety of systems, and explores several radio and infrared light technologies.

Wireless PAN Components

Wireless PANs make use of both radio and infrared light technologies, which manufacturers embed in many different types of devices.

User Devices

Wireless PANs don't require much battery power to operate, making them ideal for small user devices, such as audio headsets, cell phones, PDAs, game controls, GPS units, digital cameras, and laptops. Figure 4-1 illustrates several of these types of devices. For example, a wireless PAN enables someone to listen to music on headsets wirelessly from their PDA. Or a person can transfer his phone book from his laptop to a cell phone. As with these cases, wireless PANs eliminate wires that often frustrate users.

Figure 4-1   Many Different Types of User Devices Operate on Wireless PANs

Radio NICs

Radio NICs are available for wireless PANs in PC Card and Compact Flash (CF) form factors. If you have a laptop, for example, it's easy to add wireless PAN connectivity by installing a PC Card. These products are available from different vendors. Many of the newer PDAs and laptops come equipped with one or more wireless PAN interfaces. This makes these wireless devices ready to connect with other devices, such as printers, PDAs, and cell phones that also have wireless PAN interfaces. The larger PC Cards are uncommon for wireless PANs, mainly because wireless PAN technologies are ideal for small devices.

USB Adapters

Several companies offer a wireless PAN USB adapter (see Figure 4-2), which is also called a wireless dongle. For example, you can purchase a USB Bluetooth adapter and connect it to a USB port on your PC. This makes the PC able to synchronize with other devices having Bluetooth connectivity. Bluetooth—which is discussed later—is a specification developed for short-range, radio-based transceivers.

Figure 4-2   Bluetooth Wireless USB Adapters Enable PCs and
                    Laptops to Interface with other Bluetooth Devices

A PDA utilizing Bluetooth can wirelessly interface with the Bluetooth-enabled
PC and synchronize without placing the PDA in a synchronization cradle. A USB
connection over Bluetooth, however, is generally slower than having a directly
wired interface through the PC's USB port. This is because the wireless USB
adapter is mapped to the PC's serial port, which runs slower than the USB port.
The wireless solution might be more convenient, but you might need to wait twice
as long before synchronization is complete.

Routers

Most wireless PAN applications simply involve cable replacement, but some vendors sell Bluetooth-equipped routers to support wireless connections to the Internet. Because of limited range, though, these wireless PAN routers are primarily
for home and small office use. In order to satisfy more connectivity needs, some
wireless PAN routers also support wireless LAN interfaces, such as 802.11.

Wireless PAN Systems

Wireless PAN systems generally apply to individual users, and some offer support
for multiple users. Take a closer look at several wireless PAN system configurations.

Home and Small Office

Many different system configurations of wireless PANs exist in the home and small office.

Synchronization

One of the most common uses of wireless PANs is PDA and cell phone synchronization with a laptop or PC. Figure 4-3 illustrates the interconnection of components for this type of system. When the user presses a sync button on the handheld device, the radio NIC within the handheld device sends the corresponding data to the radio NIC in the laptop or PC. Likewise, the laptop or PC will send data to the handheld device. In most cases, the wireless connection extends the serial RS-232 port wirelessly to the handheld device.

Figure 4-3   Synchronization Transfers Information in Both
Directions Between Two Devices

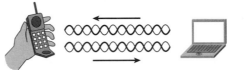

Streaming Multimedia

A large number of wireless PAN applications involve streaming audio and video. For example, a user can easily listen to streaming MP3 files stored on an MP3 player. (See Figure 4-4.) Many PDAs have the capability of playing MP3 audio files by installing one of the popular media players, such as the RealOne media player from RealNetworks, Inc. With a wireless PAN, the user doesn't need to carry around the MP3 player and mess with wires or stay within the same area to listen to music. A similar configuration involves the use of a wireless audio earpiece and microphone for a hands-free operation of a cell phone. A drawback to this approach, however, is that batteries will not last as long when using the wireless connections.

Figure 4-4   Wireless PANs Permit Easy Use of Headphones

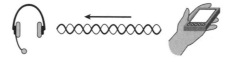

Another benefit of wireless PANs in streaming applications is flexible connectivity between video cameras and a server. A homeowner could, for example, place web cams in strategic places for security monitoring purposes. A hidden camera aimed at the front door area allows the homeowner to screen visitors before opening the door. The use of wireless, in this case, simplifies the installation because it eliminates the need to run wires to the camera. Electrical current or batteries are still necessary to power the camera, of course, but electrical outlets are available throughout a home.

Control

Wireless PANs eliminate wires for computer peripherals, such as a wireless mouse, keyboard, and telephone connection, making it easier to move and set up PCs. A user, for example, can use a full-sized keyboard wirelessly with a laptop or PDA. In addition, wireless PANs reduce the tangle of cables surrounding a desktop computer. Reliability is higher because of less cable breakage and less risk of someone inadvertently kicking a cable loose.

Printing

Wireless connections between your PC and printer are made possible within the same room through a wireless PAN connection. (See Figure 4-5.) Printer cables are often too short, and you're stuck setting the printer in a less than ideal location. The wireless PAN connection allows the movement of the printer to a better location.

Figure 4-5   Printing Is Easy with a Wireless PAN

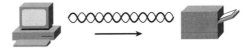

Internet Connections

A user can access e-mail and browse the web from anywhere within the room
with a wireless PAN interface to the Internet. Instead of sitting at a desk, for
example, a person can relax in a lounge chair or couch. This freedom makes computing much more enjoyable. Figure 4-6 shows the system configuration that
makes this possible.

Figure 4-6   A Wireless PAN Router Allows Connectivity to the Internet

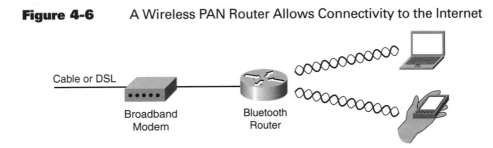

Enterprise

The use of wireless PANs in enterprise is common; however, the applications and
system configurations are similar to homes and small offices. Employees use
wireless PANs to synchronize PDAs with desktop computers and take advantage
of wireless peripherals. Instead of using a wireless PAN router for connecting
users to the Internet however, an enterprise makes use of wireless LANs for Internet connectivity. Enterprises span too large of an area to make wireless PANs
practical because of the rather large number of required base stations.

Wireless PAN Technologies

Wireless PAN technologies utilize both radio frequencies and infrared light, depending on the application.

802.15

The IEEE 802.15 standards working group focuses on the development of standards for wireless PANs and coordinates with other standards, such as 802.11 wireless LANs.

The 802.15 standards working group contains the following elements:

- **802.15.1**—This working group, Task Group 1, defines a wireless PAN standard based on Bluetooth v1.1 specifications, which uses frequency hopping spread spectrum (FHSS) and operates at up to 1 Mbps. The 802.15 group published 802.11.1 in June of 2002, and it is meant to serve as a resource for developers of Bluetooth devices.

- **802.15.2**—The group responsible for this standard, Task Group 2, is defining recommended practices to facilitate the coexistence of 802.15 and 802.11 networks. An issue is that both networks operate in the same 2.4 GHz frequency band, making coordination between operations necessary. The group is quantifying the interference and proposing methods to counter the interference.

- **802.15.3**—This is Task Group 3, which is drafting a new standard for higher-rate wireless PANs. Data rates include 11, 22, 33, 44, and 55 Mbps. Combined with these higher data rates, quality of service (QoS) mechanisms make this standard good for satisfying needs for multimedia applications. This group is also focusing on lower cost and power requirements. A draft of the 802.15.3 standard is now available for purchase.

- **802.15.4**—This group, Task Group 4, is investigating the definition of a standard with low data rates that leads to extremely low-power consumption for small devices where it's not practical to change batteries within months or years. For example, sensors, smart badges, and home automation systems are candidates for this technology. Data rates include 20, 40, and 250 kbps. A draft of the 802.15.4 standard is now available for purchase.

note

For more information and updates regarding the 802.15 standard, refer to http://grouper.ieee.org/groups/802/15/.

Bluetooth

The introduction of Bluetooth in 1998 was the result of several companies, including Ericsson, IBM, Intel, Nokia, and Toshiba, working together to create a solution for wireless access among computing devices. Bluetooth, which is a specification and not a standard, is ideal for small devices with short-range, low-power, and inexpensive radio links. This makes Bluetooth a good solution for connecting small devices within range of a person in a small working area. That's why the 802.15 chose Bluetooth as the basis of the 802.15.1 standard.

Basic Features

The Bluetooth Special Interest Group (SIG) published the initial version of the specification in mid-1999. There have been updates since then, but the technical attributes are essentially the same. Bluetooth transceivers operate at up to 1 Mbps data rate in the 2.4GHz band, using FHSS technology. It constantly hops over the entire spectrum at a rate of 1,600 hops per second, which is much faster than the 802.11 version of frequency hopping.

Low-power Bluetooth devices have a range of 30 feet. High-power Bluetooth devices, however, can reach distances of around 300 feet. The high-power mode, though, is rare.

Bluetooth modules have relatively small form factors. Typical measurements are $10.2 \times 14 \times 1.6$ millimeters, which is small enough to fit in a variety of user devices.

Bluetooth enables automatic connection among Bluetooth devices that fall within range of each other, but a user has the ability to accept and disallow connections with specific users. Users, however, should always be aware of whether their

Bluetooth connection is enabled. To ensure security, disable the Bluetooth connection. Encryption is also part of the specification.

Could Bluetooth Replace Wireless LANs?

Bluetooth has characteristics similar to wireless LANs. Through the use of the high-power version of Bluetooth, manufacturers can develop Bluetooth access points and routers with a similar range as 802.11 networks. The current Bluetooth products, however, are mostly low power and focus on wireless PAN functions. In addition, it would be difficult for any Bluetooth wireless LAN products to gain a strong foothold in the market because 802.11 products already have widespread adoption.

The place where Bluetooth falls behind 802.11 is performance and range. 802.11 components can reach data rates of up to 54 Mbps, while Bluetooth lags way behind at around 1 Mbps. This might be good enough for most cable replacement applications— such as an interface between headphones and a PDA— but higher performance is necessary when surfing the web through a broadband connection or participating on a corporate network. Also, the range of 802.11 is typically 300 feet inside offices, which is much greater than Bluetooth. Bluetooth would require many access points to fully cover larger areas.

As a result, it's highly unlikely that Bluetooth products will win over 802.11. This is certainly apparent because electronics stores primarily sell 802.11 (Wi-Fi) solutions for wireless LAN applications, not Bluetooth.

Could Wireless LANs Replace Bluetooth?

It's possible that 802.11 wireless LANs could have a big impact on the sale of Bluetooth devices, mostly because 802.11 meets or exceeds nearly all of the characteristics of Bluetooth. Because widespread adoption of Bluetooth is still lacking, there's time for 802.11 vendors to get their foot in the door with manufacturers needing support for wireless PANs.

Some modifications would need to be made, however. The size of 802.11 components needs to be smaller, but that is becoming more of a reality as semiconductor companies strive for miniaturization of their 802.11 chipsets. These smaller components require less power, making them more competitive for devices, such as mobile phones, that have smaller batteries. With the 802.15 group defining standards for wireless PANs based on Bluetooth— and the 802.11 group focusing on wireless LANs— it's likely that both Bluetooth and 802.11 will continue to coexist and complement each other.

Minimizing Bluetooth Interference

As more wireless products become available, you need to carefully manage potential frequency interference. Tests have shown significant interference between Bluetooth and other systems operating in the 2.4 GHz band, such as 802.11 wireless LANs. A critical problem is that Bluetooth and 802.11b neither understand each other nor follow the same rules. A Bluetooth radio might haphazardly begin transmitting data while an 802.11 station is sending a frame. This results in a collision, which forces the 802.11 station to retransmit the frame. This lack of coordination is the basis for radio frequency (RF) interference between Bluetooth and 802.11.

Because of the potential for collisions, 802.11 and Bluetooth networks suffer from lower performance. An 802.11 station automatically lowers its data rate and retransmits a frame when collisions occur. Consequently, the 802.11 protocol introduces delays in the presence of Bluetooth interference.

The full impact of RF interference depends on the utilization and proximity of Bluetooth devices. Interference occurs only when both Bluetooth and 802.11b devices transmit at the same time. Users might have Bluetooth devices in their PDAs or laptops, but no interference will exist if their applications are not using the Bluetooth radio to send data.

Some Bluetooth applications, such as printing from a laptop or synchronizing a PDA to a desktop, utilize the radio for a short period of time. In this case, the Bluetooth devices are not active long enough to noticeably degrade the performance of an 802.11 network. For example, a user might synchronize her PDA to her desktop when arriving at work in the morning. Other than that, their Bluetooth radio might be inactive and not cause interference the rest of the day.

The biggest impact is when a company implements a large-scale Bluetooth network, such as one that enables mobility for doctors and nurses using PDAs throughout a hospital. If the Bluetooth network is widespread and under moderate-to-high levels of utilization, the Bluetooth system will probably offer a substantial number of collisions with an 802.11 network residing in the same area. In this case, Bluetooth and 802.11 would have difficulties coexisting, and performance would likely suffer.

In addition to utilization, the proximity of the Bluetooth devices to 802.11 radio NICs and access points has a tremendous affect on the degree of interference. The transmit power of Bluetooth devices is generally lower than 802.11 wireless LANs. Therefore, an 802.11 station must be relatively close (within 10 feet or so) of a transmitting Bluetooth device before significant interference can occur.

A typical application fitting this scenario is a laptop user utilizing Bluetooth to support connections to a PDA and printer and 802.11 to access the Internet and corporate servers. The potential for interference in this situation is enormous, especially when the user is operating within outer limits of the coverage area of the 802.11 network. Figure 4-7 illustrates this situation. The signal from the Bluetooth device will likely drown out the weaker 802.11 signal because of the distance of the access point.

Figure 4-7   RF Interference Can Occur Between Bluetooth and 802.11
Wireless LAN Devices

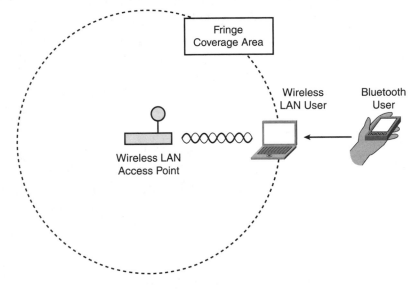

Here are some tips on how to avoid interference from Bluetooth devices:

■ **Manage the use of RF devices**—One way to reduce the potential for interference is to regulate the types of RF devices within your home or office. In other words, establish your own private regulatory body for managing unlicensed RF devices. The extreme measure would be to completely ban the use of Bluetooth; however, that is not practical or even possible in all cases. For example, you can't feasibly prohibit the use of Bluetooth in public areas of large offices. For private applications, you could set company policies to limit the use of Bluetooth to specific applications, such as synchronizing PDAs to desktops.

■ **Ensure adequate 802.11 coverage**—Strong, healthy 802.11 signals throughout the coverage areas reduce the impact of the Bluetooth signals. If wireless LAN transmissions become too weak, the interfering Bluetooth signals will be more troublesome. Perform a thorough RF site survey, and determine the appropriate location for access points.

- **Move to the 5 GHz band**—If none of the preceding steps solve the problem, consider using a 5 GHz wireless LAN such as 802.11a. You can completely avoid RF interference in this band— at least for the foreseeable future.

note

For more information about the Bluetooth specification and related products, refer to http://www.bluetooth.com.

IrDA

Bluetooth's primary competitor is *Infrared Data Association (IrDA)*, which has been defining and publishing since 1993. The IrDA has a charter to create an interoperable, low-cost, low-power, serial data communications standard for short-range applications. IrDA has been around for much longer than Bluetooth. In fact, many laptops and cell phones have been coming equipped with an IrDA interface for years.

Basic Features

The basis for IrDA is infrared light, which doesn't go through walls and other obstacles. This strictly limits the range of IrDA devices to within an obstacle-free room. This makes IrDA useful only for point-to-point applications, such as synchronizing PDAs to PCs. An advantage of IrDA, however, is that there's no worry about RF interference.

The IrDA data standard, which is best for devices such as an MP3 player needing to stream information, offers up to 4 Mbps data rates. This version of the standard has up to 3 feet (1 meter range), but low-power versions significantly conserve battery power and reduce operation to approximately 8 inches (20 centimeters).

To effectively support wireless computer peripherals, such as a keyboard or mouse, the IrDA control version of the standard reduces data rates to 75 kbps. In addition, the host computer can communicate with up to eight peripherals simultaneously.

note

For more information regarding the IrDA specification and related products, refer to http://www.irda.org.

Chapter Summary

Wireless PANs are meant to provide wireless network connections in small areas, such as within a room. Devices equipped with Bluetooth or IrDA significantly reduce cables, which increases the flexibility of applications— such as hands-free operation of cell phones, listening to streaming audio players, and synchronizing a PDA to a computer. Many of the types of applications fall within both home and enterprise.

Bluetooth and IrDA are the primary technologies that wireless PANs implement. The 802.15 group elected the use of Bluetooth as the basis for the 802.15.1 standard for wireless PANs. Because of limited range and performance of Bluetooth, it's not likely that wireless PANs will replace 802.11 wireless LANs.

Chapter Review Questions

You can find the answers to the following questions in Appendix A, "Answers to Chapter Review Questions."

1. What form factors are common for wireless PAN radio cards?

2. What application can strongly benefit through the use of a wireless USB adapter (also referred to as a wireless dongle)?

3. When would the use of a wireless PAN router make sense?

4. What is the general maximum coverage area of a wireless PAN?

5. Which IEEE standards group uses Bluetooth as the basis for the standard?

6. In what frequency band does Bluetooth operate?

7. What is the primary issue of using Bluetooth around 802.11 wireless LANs?

8. A Bluetooth-enabled device is always transmitting. True or false?

9. What is the highest possible data rate of an IrDA device?

10. What is a benefit of IrDA as compared to Bluetooth?

What You Will Learn

After reading this chapter, you should be able to

- ✔ Recognize specific wireless LAN applications

- ✔ Understand wireless LAN components and standards

- ✔ Understand the configuration of wireless LAN systems

CHAPTER 5

Wireless LANs: Networks for Buildings and Campuses

Wireless LANs effectively satisfy needs within buildings and campus environments. With performance and security comparable to wired networks, wireless LAN solutions are found in homes, small offices, enterprises, and public areas. Wireless LANs are able to support many different types of applications.

This chapter defines each of the primary wireless LAN components, describes how these components interconnect to form a variety of systems, and explores the 802.11 standards.

Wireless LAN Components

Wireless LANs consist of components similar to traditional Ethernet-wired LANs. In fact, wireless LAN protocols are similar to Ethernet and comply with the same form factors. The big difference, however, is that wireless LANs don't require wires.

User Devices

Users of wireless LANs operate a multitude of devices, such as PCs, laptops, and PDAs. The use of wireless LANs to network stationary PCs is beneficial because of limited needs for wiring. Laptops and PDAs, however, are commonly equipped with wireless LAN connectivity because of their portable nature. User devices might consist of specialized hardware as well. For example, bar code scanners and patient monitoring devices often have wireless LAN connectivity.

Radio NICs

A major part of a wireless LAN includes a radio NIC that operates within the computer device and provides wireless connectivity. A wireless LAN radio NIC, sometimes referred to as a radio card, often implements the 802.11 standard. The cards generally implement one particular physical layer, such as 802.11a or 802.11b/g. As a result, the radio card must utilize a version of the standard that is compatible with the wireless LAN. Wireless LAN radio cards that implement multiple versions of the standard and provide better *interoperability* are becoming more common.

Radio cards come in a variety of form factors, including: ISA, PCI, PC card, mini-PCI, and CF. PCs generally utilize ISA and PCI cards; but PDAs and laptops use PC cards, mini-PCI, and CF adapters.

Access Points

An access point contains a radio card that communicates with individual user devices on the wireless LAN, as well as a wired NIC that interfaces to a *distribution system*, such as Ethernet. System software within the access point bridges together the wireless LAN and distribution sides of the access point. The system software differentiates access points by providing varying degrees of management, installation, and security functions. Figure 5-1 shows an example of access-point hardware.

Figure 5-1   Wireless LAN Access Points Connect Wireless LANs to Wired Networks (Photo Courtesy of Linksys)

In most cases, the access point provides an http interface that enables configuration changes to the access point through an end-user device that is equipped with a network interface and a web browser. Some access points also have a serial RS-232 interface for configuring the access point through a serial cable as well as a user device running terminal emulation and Telnet software, such as hyper terminal.

Configuring an Access Point

Look at the basic radio configuration settings for a Cisco 350 access point. These types of settings are common for other access points as well.

One parameter that you should set is the service set identifier (SSID). The SSID provides a name for the specific wireless LAN that users will associate with. For security purposes, it's a good idea to set the SSID to something other than the default value.

For most applications, set the transmit power of the access point to the highest value, which is typically 100 milliwatt (mW) in the United States. This will maximize the range of the wireless LAN. The actual maximum effective power output is 1 watt, but the lower transmit power allows enough margin to allow the use of a higher-gain antenna and still remain within limitations.

In the United States, set the access point to operate on any one of the channels in the range from 1 through 11. When installing only one access point, it doesn't matter which channel you choose. If you install multiple access points, or you know of a nearby wireless LAN within range of yours, you need to select different non-overlapping channels (such as channels 1, 6, and 11) for each access point within range of one another.

As a minimum, activate wired equivalent privacy (WEP) encryption as a minimum level of security. You'll need to assign an encryption key that all user devices will need in order to interface with the access point with encrypted data. If you choose to implement 40-bit keys, enter 10 hexadecimal characters, with each character having the value of 1 through 9 or A through F. The 104-bit keys require 26 hexadecimal characters. Keep in mind that 40-bit keys correspond with 64-bit encryption and 104-bit keys correspond with 128-bit encryption to the addition of a 24-bit initialization vector in both cases.

Routers

By definition, a router transfers packets between networks. The router chooses the next best link to send packets on to get closer to the destination. Routers use *Internet Protocol (IP)* packet headers and routing tables, as well as internal protocols, to determine the best path for each packet.

A wireless LAN router adds a built-in access point function to a multiport Ethernet router. This combines multiple Ethernet networks with wireless connections. A typical wireless LAN router includes four Ethernet ports, an 802.11 access point, and sometimes a parallel port so it can be a print server. This gives wireless users the same ability as wired users to send and receive packets over multiple networks.

Routers implement the *Network Address Translation (NAT)* protocol that enables multiple network devices to share a single *IP address* provided by an Internet service provider (ISP). Figure 5-2 illustrates this concept. Routers also implement *Dynamic Host Configuration Protocol (DHCP)* services for all devices. DHCP assigns private IP addresses to devices. Together, NAT and DHCP make it possible for several network devices, such as PCs, laptops, and printers to share a common Internet IP address.

Figure 5-2   NAT and DHCP Are Essential Protocols That Routers Implement

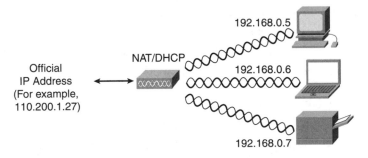

Wireless LAN routers offer strong benefits in the home and small office setting. For example, you can subscribe to a cable modem service that provides a single IP address through DHCP to the router, and the router then provides IP addresses through DHCP to clients on your local network. NAT then maps a particular client on the local network to the ISP-assigned IP address whenever that client needs to access the Internet. As a result, you need a router if you plan to have more than one networked device on a local network sharing a single ISP-assigned address. Instead of having one box for the router and another box for the access point, a wireless LAN router provides both in the same box. Routers, however, are seldom used in larger implementations, such as hospitals and company headquarters. In these cases, access points are best because the network will have existing wired components that deal with IP addresses.

Repeaters

Access points, which require interconnecting cabling, generally play a dominant role for providing coverage in most wireless LAN deployments. Wireless *repeaters*, however, are a way to extend the range of an existing wireless LAN instead of adding more access points. There are few standalone wireless LAN repeaters on the market, but some access points have a built-in repeater mode.

A repeater simply regenerates a network signal to extend the range of the existing network infrastructure. (See Figure 5-3.) A wireless LAN repeater does not physically connect by wire to any part of the network. Instead, it receives radio signals from an access point, end-user device, or another repeater; it retransmits the frames. This makes it possible for a repeater located between an access point and distant user to act as a relay for frames traveling back and forth between the user and the access point.

Figure 5-3   Wireless LAN Repeaters Are Simple Devices That Require No Cabling

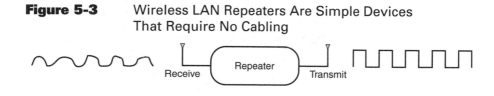

As a result, wireless repeaters are an effective solution to overcome signal impairments such as RF attenuation. For example, repeaters provide connectivity to remote areas that normally would not have wireless network access. An access point in a home or small office might not quite cover the entire area where users need connectivity, such as a basement or patio. The placement of a repeater between the covered and uncovered areas, however, will provide connectivity throughout the entire space. The wireless repeater fills holes in coverage, enabling seamless roaming.

A downside of wireless repeaters, however, is that they reduce performance of a wireless LAN. A repeater must receive and retransmit each frame on the same radio channel, which effectively doubles the amount of traffic on the network. This problem compounds when using multiple repeaters, because each repeater will duplicate the data sent. Therefore, be sure to plan the use of repeaters sparingly.

Antennae

Most antennae for wireless LANs are omnidirectional and have low gain. Nearly all access points, routers, and repeaters come standard with omnidirectional antennae. Omnidirectional antennae satisfy most coverage requirements; however, consider the use of optional directive antennae to cover a long, narrow area. In some cases, the antenna is integrated within a radio card or access point and there is no choice to make. If a need exists to use a directive antenna (higher gain), ensure that the radio card or access point has an external antenna connector.

Wireless LAN Systems

A wireless LAN system consists of a set of components and configurations that satisfy the needs of a particular application. It's possible to define a general wireless LAN system based on broad application types. Take a look at some examples.

Home and Small Office Wireless LANs

The use of a wireless LAN in a home or small office avoids the need to run network cabling to interconnect PCs, laptops, and printers. Just about anyone can purchase applicable components at an electronics or office supply store and install a wireless LAN. Installation and configuration of the wireless LAN is simple.

As shown in Figure 5-4, a home or small office wireless LAN generally includes a single wireless LAN router that connects to a broadband Internet connection, such as DSL or cable modem. The typical range of a wireless LAN router is adequate to cover a house, apartment, or small office. A router is necessary if there is more than one network device. For example, a home consisting of one wireless PC, a laptop, and a printer requires NAT and DHCP to satisfy the addressing needs of all devices.

Figure 5-4   Wireless LANs in Home or Small Offices Have a Simple Configuration

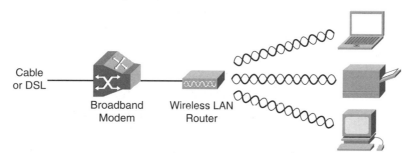

Cable or DSL — Broadband Modem — Wireless LAN Router

An access point alone will also work in a home or small office, but it will allow only one network device to obtain an IP address and access the Internet. This occurs because most access points do not implement DHCP and NAT. The combination of an access point and wired router (see Figure 5-5), however, will suffice for a wireless LAN router. This might be a less expensive solution than purchasing a wireless LAN router if you already own an access point or wired router (or both).

Figure 5-5   Combining a Wireless LAN Access Point and an Ethernet Router Offers the Same Functionality of a Wireless LAN Router

Ethernet
Router

Wireless LAN
Access Point

tip

Wireless LAN access points and routers have default security settings, such as WEP, initially turned off. To prevent someone outside your home or office from accessing files on your network, activate security controls when setting up the wireless LAN.

Enterprise Wireless LANs

A wireless LAN for an enterprise is much more complicated than for homes and small offices. The main reason is that enterprise wireless LANs require multiple access points with the need of a substantial distribution system that interconnects the access points. As show in Figure 5-6, the access points offer overlapping radio cells that enable users to roam through a facility and access resources on a wired network. This configuration, often referred to as infrastructure mode, is the most common for any wireless LAN needing to cover an area greater than 20,000 square feet.

Figure 5-6   Enterprise Wireless LANs Require a Substantial Amount of Cabling to Interconnect Access Points

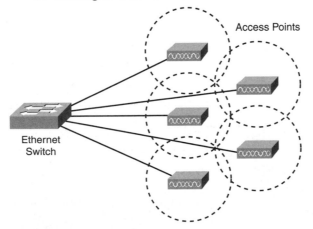

Access Points

Ethernet
Switch

For example, a wireless LAN for a hospital might consist of hundreds of access points located throughout the hospital. A large array of Ethernet switches and associated cabling would be necessary to tie everything together. As with other enterprise wireless LANs, a hospital will likely have existing hardware that provides DHCP services. As a result, an enterprise wireless LAN utilizes access points, not wireless LAN routers.

Enterprise wireless LANs also require sophisticated security mechanisms. More emphasis must be placed on authentication and encryption than what is necessary for home and small office applications. Read Chapter 8, "Wireless Network Security: Protecting Information Resources," for more details on wireless LAN security.

tip

When deploying an enterprise or public wireless LAN, be certain to have a wireless LAN specialist perform an RF site survey to assess the presence of RF interference sources an and determine the optimum placement of access points and RF channel assignments.

Wireless LANs Good for Patients

Health-care centers, such as hospitals and doctors' offices, must maintain accurate records to ensure effective patient care. A simple mistake can cost someone's life. As a result, doctors and nurses must carefully record test results, physical data, pharmaceutical orders, and surgical procedures. This paperwork often overwhelms health-care staff, taking 50 to 70 percent of their time. The use of a mobile data collection device that wirelessly transmits the data to a centralized database significantly increases accuracy and raises the visibility of the data to those who need the information. This results in better care given to patients.

Doctors and nurses are also extremely mobile, going from room to room caring for patients. The use of electronic patient records, with the ability to input, view, and update patient data from anywhere in the hospital, increases the accuracy and speed of health care. This improvement is possible by providing each nurse and doctor with a wireless pen-based computer, such as a tablet or PDA, coupled with a wireless network to databases that store critical medical information about the patients.

A doctor caring for someone in the hospital, for example, can place an order for a blood test by keying the request into a handheld computer. The laboratory will receive the order electronically and dispatch a lab technician to draw blood from the patient. The laboratory will run the tests requested by the doctor and enter the results into the patient's electronic medical record. The doctor can then check the results through the handheld appliance from anywhere in the hospital.

Another application for wireless networks in hospitals is the tracking of pharmaceuticals. The use of mobile handheld bar code printing and scanning devices dramatically increases the efficiency and accuracy of all drug transactions, such as receiving, picking, dispensing, inventory taking, and the tracking of drug expiration dates. Most importantly, however, it ensures that hospital staff is able to administer the right drug to the right person in a timely fashion. This would not be possible without the use of wireless networks to support a centralized database and mobile data collection devices.

Public Wireless LANs

A *public wireless LAN* enables anyone with a wireless LAN NIC-equipped user device to access the Internet. Public wireless LANs are available from most hotpots, such as airports, convention centers, hotels, and marinas throughout the world. Good *hotspots* include those where people visit regularly on a temporary basis and want access to network services.

 note
Locate a nearby public wireless LAN hotspot at
http://www.wi-fihotspotlist.com/.

A public wireless LAN is one that anyone can use. This provides a source of revenue because the hotspot owner can bill subscribers. In some situations, though, hotspot owners offer free access in order to increase the use of their establishment.

Wireless LANs for small hotspots are simple. For example, a coffee shop owner can install a single wireless LAN router that interfaces to a broadband Internet connection. This configuration is similar to one needed for a home or small office. Free access encourages patrons to purchase coffee and other goodies as they surf the web and correspond with e-mail.

In cases where the hotspot owner wants to charge for access, then the wireless LAN system needs to include an access controller and billing function as shown in Figure 5-7. When a user runs her web browser, the access controller automatically redirects her to a web page that prompts the user to log in or sign up for service. Billing options include per-minute, per-day, or per-month plans. The billing system keeps track of usage and automatically charges credit cards.

Figure 5-7   Public Wireless LANs Require Components That Fall Outside the Scope of Wireless Networking Technologies

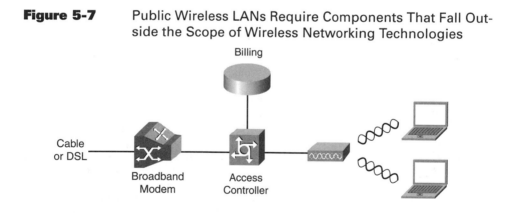

Large hotspots require multiple access points, comparable to an enterprise wireless LAN. Public wireless LANs spanning several locations, however, also requires rather sophisticated access control and billing systems. A large hotel chain, for example, might deploy public wireless LANs at a hundred different locations. Users can subscribe for months of access and be able to use the service from any of the hotels. The access control function in this situation requires a centralized server that maintains authentication, authorization, and accounting (AAA) information.

Wireless LANs in Hotels

To offer wireless coverage for their patrons, hotels have been installing access points in convention centers, ballrooms, meeting rooms, lobbies, swimming pool areas, and guest rooms.

A hotel wireless LAN can enable guests to do all of the following during their stay:

- Browse the Web at the pool or in the fitness center.

- Remotely and securely access their corporate networks from their room.

- Review online schedules and get driving directions.

- Share a high-speed Internet connection with multiple conference participants.

- Remotely print from guest rooms to printers in the business center.

- Conduct video conferences with associates or family members.

The staff and management of hotels can also reap huge benefits from wireless LANs. For example, the deployment of a wireless LAN makes the following tasks much easier and efficient:

- Conduct room inspections to see if everything is in order and no damage was done to the room after guests check out of the hotel. The staff can check the room and send feedback to the main computer through an 802.11-enabled PDA.

- Perform security and safety inspections to make sure doors are locked, fire extinguishers are charged, emergency lights are in working order, and so on. All of the information is updated in real time, saving time and the possibility of error.

- Keep in contact with maintenance workers by using wireless LAN phones. Management can contact maintenance whenever needed, resulting in quicker response times.

Ad Hoc Wireless LANs

An ad hoc wireless LAN, as Figure 5-8 illustrates, does not utilize access points. Instead, each individual user device communicates directly with another user device. The advantage of this configuration is that users can spontaneously form a wireless LAN quickly. Ad hoc networks are also commonly referred to as peer-to-peer networks.

Figure 5-8   Ad Hoc Wireless LANs Offer Simple Setup and Operation

For example, an ad hoc wireless LAN makes it easy for someone to transfer a large file to an associate in a conference room where an infrastructure wireless LAN is not available. Each user simply configures his radio NIC to operate in *ad hoc mode*, and connections are made automatically. In some cases, the users need to ensure that their IP addresses are set within the same subnet.

Ad hoc mode is also beneficial for supporting emergency services where operations might take place in areas where a wired distribution system for interconnecting access points is not practical. A disaster relief group, for example, can quickly set up network connections among staff working in areas afflicted by hurricanes, floods, and terrorist attacks.

Wireless LAN Technologies

802.11 and HiperLAN/2 are the most common standards for wireless LANs. Examine each of these standards.

802.11

The IEEE 802.11 standard specifies a common *medium access control (MAC)* and several physical layers for wireless LANs. The initial 802.11 standard became available in 1997, but wireless LANs didn't begin to proliferate on a large scale until 2001, when prices fell dramatically. The IEEE 802.11 working group actively continues to enhance the standard to improve the performance and security of wireless LANs.

note

The 802.11 standard specifies use of an infrared light physical layer; however, no products on the market today comply with this version of the standard.

802.11 MAC Layer

The 802.11 standard specifies a single MAC Layer, which provides a variety of functions that support the operation of 802.11-based wireless LANs. The MAC Layer manages and maintains communications between 802.11 stations (radio network cards and access points) by coordinating access to the shared air medium. Often viewed as the brains of the network, the 802.11 MAC Layer directs a particular 802.11 Physical layer, such as 802.11a, 802.11b, or 802.11g, to perform the tasks of sensing the medium, transmission, and receiving of 802.11 frames.

Before transmitting frames, a station must first gain access to the medium, which is a radio channel that stations share. The 802.11 standard defines two forms of medium access: *distributed coordination function (DCF)* and point coordination function (PCF). DCF is mandatory and based on the CSMA/CA (*carrier sense multiple access* with collision avoidance) protocol. With DCF, 802.11 stations contend for access and attempt to send frames when there is no other station transmitting. (See Figure 5-9.) If another station is sending a frame, stations wait until the channel is free.

Figure 5-9   DCF Offers a Distributed Form of Medium Access

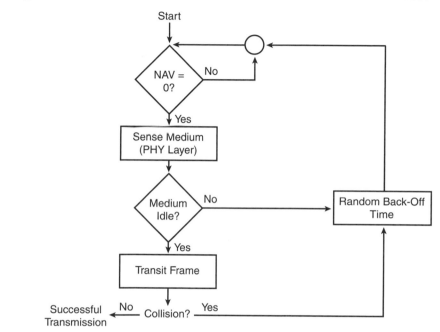

As a condition to accessing the medium (see Figure 5-9), the MAC Layer checks the value of its network allocation vector (NAV), which is a counter resident at each station that represents the amount of time that the previous frame needs to be sent. The NAV must be 0 before a station can attempt to send a frame. Prior to transmitting a frame, a station calculates the amount of time necessary to send the frame based on the its length and data rate. The station places a value representing this time in the duration field in the header of the frame. When stations receive the frame, they examine this duration field value and use it as the basis for setting their corresponding NAVs. This process reserves the medium for the sending station.

An important aspect of the DCF is a random back-off timer that a station uses if it detects a busy medium. If the channel is in use, the station must wait a random period of time before attempting to access the medium again. This ensures that multiple stations wanting to send data don't transmit at the same time. The random delay causes stations to wait different periods of time and avoids all of them sensing the medium at exactly the same time, finding the channel idle, transmitting, and colliding with each other. The back-off timer significantly reduces the number of collisions and corresponding retransmissions, especially when the number of active users increases.

With radio-based LANs, a transmitting station can't listen for collisions while sending data, mainly because the station can't have its receiver on while transmitting the frame. As a result, the receiving station needs to send an acknowledgement (ACK) if it detects no errors in the received frame. If the sending station doesn't receive an ACK after a specified period of time, the sending station assumes that there was a collision (or RF interference) and retransmits the frame.

For supporting time-bounded delivery of data frames such as video, the 802.11 standard defines the optional PCF where the access point grants access to an individual station to the medium by polling the station during the contention-free period. Stations can't transmit frames unless the access point polls them first. The period of time for PCF-based data traffic (if enabled) occurs alternately between contention periods.

An access point polls stations according to a polling list, then switches to a contention period when stations use DCF. This process enables support for both synchronous and asynchronous modes of operation. No known wireless NICs or access points on the market today, however, implement PCF.

An issue with PCF is that not many vendors support it in their products. As a result, it's generally not an option available to users. Future products, however, might support PCF in order to offer quality of service (QoS) mechanisms.

The following sections summarize primary 802.11 MAC functions.

Scanning

The 802.11 standard defines both passive and active scanning, whereby a radio NIC searches for access points. Passive scanning is mandatory where each NIC scans individual channels to find the best access-point signal. Periodically, access points broadcast a beacon, and the radio NIC receives these beacons while scanning and takes note of the corresponding signal strengths. The beacons contain information about the access point, including SSID and supported data rates. The radio NIC can use this information along with the signal strength to compare access points and decide on which one to use.

Optional active scanning is similar, except the radio NIC initiates the process by broadcasting a probe frame, and all access points within range respond with a probe response. Active scanning enables a radio NIC to receive immediate response from access points, without waiting for a beacon transmission. The issue, however, is that active scanning imposes additional overhead on the network because of the transmission of probe and corresponding response frames.

Stations set to ad hoc mode form are what the 802.11 standard refers to as an independent basic service set. In this mode, one of the stations always sends a beacon, which alerts new stations of the network presence. The responsibility of transmitting the beacon is based upon each station waiting for a beacon interval to expire and an additional random time. A station transmits a beacon if after the beacon interval and random time the station does not receive a beacon from another station. This distributes the responsibility for sending beacons among all stations.

Authentication

Authentication is the process of proving identity, and the 802.11 standard specifies two forms: open system authentication and shared key authentication. Open system authentication is mandatory, and it's a two-step process. A radio NIC initiates the process by sending an authentication request frame to the access point. The access point replies with an authentication response frame containing approval or disapproval of authentication indicated in the status code field in the frame body.

Shared key authentication is an optional four-step process that bases authentication on whether the authenticating device has the correct WEP key. The radio NIC starts by sending an authentication request frame to the access point. The access point then places challenge text into the frame body of a response frame and sends it to the radio NIC. The radio NIC uses its WEP key to encrypt the challenge text and then sends it back to the access point in another authentication frame. The access point decrypts the challenge text and compares it to the initial text. If the text is equivalent, the access point assumes that the radio NIC has the correct key. The access point finishes the sequence by sending an authentication frame to the radio NIC with the approval or disapproval. Many hackers know how to break through shared key authentication, however, so it's not a good idea to depend on it for a high level of security.

Association

When authenticated, the radio NIC must associate with the access point before sending data frames. *Association* is necessary to synchronize the radio NIC and access point with important information, such as supported data rates. The radio NIC initiates the association by sending an association request frame containing elements such as SSID and supported data rates. The access point responds by sending an association response frame containing an association ID along with other information regarding the access point. Once the radio NIC and access point complete the association process, they can send data frames to each other.

WEP

With the optional WEP enabled, the wireless NIC encrypts the body (not the header) of each frame before transmission using a common key; and the receiving station decrypts the frame upon receipt using the common key. The 802.11 standard does not specify a key distribution method, which makes 802.11 wireless LANs vulnerable to eavesdroppers. The 802.11i version of the standard, however, is improving 802.11 security by incorporating 802.1x and stronger encryption into the standard.

RTS/CTS

The optional request-to-send and clear-to-send (RTS/CTS) function allows the access point to control use of the medium for stations activating RTS/CTS. With most radio NICs, users can set a maximum frame-length threshold for when the radio NIC activates RTS/CTS. For example, a frame length of 1,000 bytes triggers

RTS/CTS for all frames larger than 1,000 bytes. The use of RTS/CTS alleviates hidden node problems (where two or more radio NICs can't hear each other and they are associated with the same access point).

If the radio NIC activates RTS/CTS, it first sends an RTS frame to an access point before sending a data frame. The access point then responds with a CTS frame, indicating that the radio NIC can send the data frame. With the CTS frame, the access point provides a value in the duration field of the frame header that holds off other stations from transmitting until after the radio NIC initiating the RTS can send its data frame. This avoids collisions between hidden nodes. The RTS/CTS handshake continues for each frame, as long as the frame size exceeds the threshold set in the corresponding radio NIC.

Power Save Mode

The optional power save mode that a user can turn on enables the radio NIC to conserve battery power when there is no need to send data. With power save mode on, the radio NIC indicates its desire to enter a sleep state to the access point through a status bit located in the header of each frame. The access point takes note of each radio NIC wanting to enter power save mode and buffers packets corresponding to the sleeping station.

In order to still receive data frames, the sleeping NIC must wake up periodically (at the right time) to receive regular beacon transmissions coming from the access point. These beacons identify whether sleeping stations have frames buffered at the access point and are waiting for delivery to their respective destinations. The radio NICs having awaiting frames will request them from the access point. After receiving the frames, the radio NIC can go back to sleep.

Fragmentation

The optional fragmentation function enables an 802.11 station to divide data packets into smaller frames. This is to avoid needing to retransmit large frames in the presence of RF interference. The bit errors resulting from RF interference are likely to affect a single frame, and it requires less overhead to retransmit a smaller frame rather than a larger one. As with RTS/CTS, users can set a maximum frame-length threshold for when the radio NIC activates fragmentation. If the frame size is larger than the threshold, the radio NIC breaks the packet into multiple frames, with each frame no larger than the threshold value.

802.11 Physical Layers

Several 802.11 Physical layers satisfy a variety of application requirements. The following sections provide a summary of each of the 802.11 Physical layers.

Initial 802.11

The initial 802.11 standard ratified in 1997 includes *frequency hopping spread spectrum (FHSS)* and *direct sequence spread spectrum (DSSS)* physical layers operating in the 2.4-GHz band with data rates of up to 2 Mbps. FHSS transmits a wideband signal that spans the entire 2.4-GHz band. It's possible to tune FHSS access points to as many as 15 different hopping patterns that don't interfere with each other, which enables up to 15 FHSS access points to effectively operate in the same area.

Because the current version of 802.11 FHSS has only a maximum data rate of 2 Mbps, not many companies sell FHSS solutions for an indoor wireless LAN. Much faster 802.11a, 802.11b, and 802.11g wireless LANs are now available. Also, FHSS doesn't interoperate with any of the other 802.11 physical layers. FHSS does, however, provide a very solution for outdoor, point-to-multipoint systems. This is because FHSS is more resilient to the RF interference that might be present in outdoor environments.

802.11 DSSS also operates only up to 2 Mbps, but it interoperates with the newer 802.11b physical layer. As a result, a user having an 802.11 DSSS radio NIC in her laptop can interface with an 802.11b access point. This situation is unlikely, however, because 802.11 DSSS radio NICs are not sold anymore.

802.11a

Toward the end of 1999, the IEEE released 802.11a, which defines operation in the 5-GHz band using Orthogonal Frequency Division Multiplexing (OFDM) with data rates up to 54 Mbps. Products, however, didn't become available until 2000, primarily because of the difficulties in developing circuitry in the 5-GHz band.

802.11a operates up to 54 Mbps in the 5-GHz band using OFDM with a range up to 100 feet depending on the actual data rate. 802.11a access points and radio NICs just became available in late 2001; therefore, the installed base of 802.11a wireless LANs today is relatively small as compared to 802.11b. Because of this, carefully consider interoperability issues that might result if you choose to deploy 802.11a networks.

A strong advantage of 802.11a is that it offers the highest capacity because of 12 separate, non-overlapping channels. This makes it a good choice for supporting a high concentration of users and higher-performance applications, such as video streaming. In addition to outperforming 802.11b systems, 802.11a has greater capacity than 802.11g.

Another advantage of 802.11a is that the 5-GHz band is uncrowded, which enables users to achieve higher levels of performance. Most interfering devices, such as microwave ovens and cordless phones, operate in the 2.4-GHz band. With less potential for RF interference, the deployment of a wireless LAN is less risky.

A potential issue of 802.11a is limited range, mainly because of operation in the higher frequency 5-GHz band. At 54 Mbps, you'll have a range less than 100 feet in most facilities. This requires a greater number of access points to fully cover a facility, as compared to an 802.11b system.

If you compare the operation of 802.11b and 802.11a, however, an 802.11a user has a higher data rate at the same range as an 802.11b user until the 802.11a user loses connectivity. The 802.11b user, however, can continue operating at lower data rates—1 or 2 Mbps, for example—at longer ranges than 802.11a.

A definite problem is that 802.11a and 802.11b/g are not compatible. For example, a user equipped with an 802.11b radio card can't associate with an 802.11a access point. The opposite scenario also applies. Vendors are solving this problem by introducing multimode radio cards that implement both 802.11a and 802.11b.

An 802.11a modulator converts the binary signal into an analog waveform through the use of different modulation types, depending on which data rate is chosen. With 6-Mbps operation, for example, the PMD uses binary phase shift keying (BPSK), which shifts the phase of the transmit center frequency to represent different data bit patterns. The higher data rates, such as 54 Mbps, employ quadrature amplitude modulation (QAM) to represent data bits by varying the transmit center frequency with different amplitude levels in addition to phase shifts.

802.11b

Along with 802.11a, IEEE ratified 802.11b, which is a higher-rate extension to the initial direct sequence standard in the 2.4-GHz band—with data rates up to 11 Mbps. 802.11b access points and radio NICs have been available since 1999; therefore, most wireless LANs installed today are 802.11b compliant.

A significant advantage of 802.11b is its relatively long-range properties. With 802.11b, you can achieve a range of 300 feet in most indoor facilities. The superior range allows the deployment of wireless LANs with fewer access points to cover a facility as compared to 802.11a.

A disadvantage of 802.11b is that you're limited to three non-overlapping channels in the 2.4 GHz band. The 802.11 standard specifies 14 channels (only channels 1 through 11 are available in the U.S.) for configuring access points; but each channel occupies roughly one third of the overall 2.4-GHz band while transmitting a signal. Most companies utilize only channels 1, 6, and 11 to ensure access points don't interfere with each other. This limits overall capacity of 802.11b, which makes it most suitable for supporting medium performance applications, such as e-mail and web surfing.

Another disadvantage of 802.11b is the potential for RF interference from other radio devices. For example, a 2.4-GHz cordless phone severely interferes with an 802.11b wireless LAN, which significantly reduces the performance for users. Microwave ovens and other devices operating in the 2.4-GHz band can also cause interference.

802.11b uses DSSS to disperse the data frame signal over a 22-MHz portion of the 2.4-GHz frequency band. This results in greater immunity to RF interference as compared to narrowband signaling, which is why the FCC deems the operation of spread spectrum systems license free.

The 802.11b modulator converts the spread binary signal into an analog waveform through the use of different modulation types, depending on which data rate is chosen. For example with 1-Mbps operation, the PMD uses differential binary phase shift keying (DBPSK). This isn't really as complex as it sounds. The modulator merely shifts the phase of the center transmit frequency to distinguish a binary 1 from a binary 0 within the data stream.

For 2-Mbps transmission, the PMD uses differential quadrature phase shift keying (DQPSK), which is similar to DBPSK except four possible phase shifts that represents every two data bits. This is a clever process that enables the data stream to be sent at 2 Mbps while using the same amount of bandwidth as the one sent at 1 Mbps. The modulator uses similar methods for the higher 5.5-Mbps and 11-Mbps data rates.

802.11g

IEEE ratified the 802.11g standard in 2003, which is compatible with 802.11b and increases performance up to 54 Mbps in the 2.4-GHz band using OFDM.

A strong advantage of 802.11g is that it's backward compatible with 802.11b. Companies with existing 802.11b networks can generally upgrade their access points to become 802.11g compliant through simple firmware upgrades. This provides an effective migration path for wireless LANs. An issue, however, is that the presence of 802.11b client devices within an 802.11g environment requires protection mechanisms that limit the performance of the overall wireless LAN. The problem is that 802.11b devices can't understand when 802.11g devices are transmitting because of a difference in modulation types. As a result, both types of devices must announce their impending use of the medium using a commonly understood modulation type.

The disadvantages of 802.11b, such as potential for RF interference and limit of three non-overlapping channels, still apply to 802.11g because of operation in the 2.4-GHz band. As a result, 802.11g networks have capacity constraints as compared to 802.11a.

2.4 GHz or 5 GHz?

When deploying a wireless LAN, companies must make a decision on whether to use NICs and access points designed to operate in the 2.4-GHz or 5-GHz band —or both. Not too long ago, the choice of frequency band was easy, when only 2.4-GHz (802.11b) products were available. Now, 802.11b and 802.11g products are both available that operate in the 2.4-GHz band, while 802.11a uses the 5-GHz band. This can cause confusion when designing a wireless LAN, so take a look at what is necessary to consider when making this critical decision.

When assessing the pros and cons of 2.4-GHz and 5-GHz systems, be sure to first define requirements. This provides a solid basis for defining all design elements. Without firm requirements, you'll be making the choice on flimsy ground.

The following are requirements for consideration when deciding between 2.4-GHz or 5-GHz solutions:

- **Geographical Location**—Consider the geographical location of where the wireless LAN will operate. A 2.4-GHz wireless LAN has regulatory acceptance throughout most of the world; however, the use of 5 GHz for wireless LANs is somewhat limited. For example, the U.S. allows operation of 5-GHz wireless LANs, but other countries do not. Your location might require you to use the 2.4-GHz band regardless of other requirements.

- **Performance**—The 5-GHz bands have much greater spectrum available. Each of the 12 non-overlapping channels in this band has 20 MHz of bandwidth. This means significantly better performance as compared to the 2.4-GHz band. The entire 2.4-GHz band is 80 MHz wide, which allows only three non-overlapping channels. If high performance is an important requirement, lean toward the 5-GHz band.

- **Facility Size**—As frequency increases, range generally decreases. As a result, 5-GHz systems generally have less range than ones operating in the 2.4-GHz band. The selection of a 5-GHz wireless LAN could require a greater number of access points, which can result in higher costs. As a result, you might benefit by deploying 2.4-GHz systems in larger facilities unless high performance is critical. Keep in mind, however, that 5-GHz systems might have equal or even better range in some situations.

- **RF Interference**—2.4GHz wireless LANs can experience interference from cordless phones, microwaves, and other wireless LANs. The interfering signals degrade the performance of an 802.11b wireless LAN by periodically blocking users and access points from accessing the shared air medium. If it's not possible to reduce potential interference to an acceptable level, consider deploying a 5-GHz system, which is relatively free from interfering sources. There are some 5-GHz phones now on the market, but it's much more possible to avoid this interference because of the many non-overlapping channels that 802.11a offers.

- **Interoperability**—2.4-GHz and 5-GHz systems are not directly compatible, and few users and access points operate in the 5-GHz band. Consequently, it might be best to deploy a 2.4-GHz solution if you have little control over the NICs that users have in their PDAs and laptops. This applies mostly to universities and public wireless LAN hotspots. Your application might require you to implement 2.4 GHz to support the more common 802.11b-equipped users.

  Vendors, however, offer dual-band radio NICs and access points, which reduces interoperability problems. Someone equipped with a dual-band radio NIC can associate with either a 2.4-GHz (802.11b/g) or 5-GHz (802.11a) access point. As a greater number of users begin equipping their devices with the dual-band radio NICs, the interoperability issue will diminish.

- **Security**—Security of the wireless LAN is of great concern to most companies. By minimizing the propagation of radio waves outside the controlled area of a facility, a wireless network is more secure because of the reduction of the potential for eavesdropping and denial of service (DoS) attacks. As a result, 5-GHz systems can provide enhanced security over 2.4-GHz systems because of less range.

  In most cases, you'll probably determine that 2.4 GHz is the way to go for common office applications. 2.4-GHz products are certainly inexpensive and capable of supporting most application requirements. Some situations, however, benefit from the use of 5 GHz, such as densely populated environments and multimedia applications.

Wi-Fi

The Wi-Fi Alliance, which began its work known as the Wireless Ethernet Compatibility Alliance (WECA), is an international nonprofit organization focusing on the marketing and interoperability of 802.11 wireless LAN products. The Wi-Fi Alliance is the group that pushes the term Wi-Fi to cover all forms of 802.11-based wireless networking, such as 802.11a, 802.11b, 802.11g, or whatever becomes available in the future. Wi-Fi Alliance is also behind *Wi-Fi Protected Access (WPA)*, the stepping stone between the much-criticized WEP and the 802.11i security standard.

The Wi-Fi Alliance has three main goals:

- Promote Wi-Fi certification worldwide by encouraging manufacturers to follow standardized 802.11 processes in the development of wireless LAN products.

- Market Wi-Fi certified products to consumers in the home, small office, and enterprise markets.

- Test and certify Wi-Fi product interoperability.

What Wi-Fi Means

Wi-Fi certification is a process that assures interoperability between 802.11 wireless LAN equipment, including access points and radio cards complying with a variety of form factors. In order to qualify for obtaining Wi-Fi certification for products, a company must become a member of the Wi-Fi Alliance.

The Wi-Fi Alliance follows an established testing program to certify that products are interoperable with other Wi-Fi certified products. After a product successfully passes every test, the manufacturer is granted the right to use the Wi-Fi Certified logo on that particular product and its corresponding packaging and manuals.

Wi-Fi certification is meant to give consumers confidence that they are purchasing wireless LAN products that have met multivendor interoperability requirements. A Wi-Fi logo on the product means that it has met interoperability testing requirements and definitely works with other vendors' Wi-Fi–certified products.

Wi-Fi Protected Access

802.11 WEP doesn't provide enough security for most enterprise wireless LAN applications. Because of static key usage, it's fairly easy to crack WEP with off-the-shelf tools. This motivates IT managers to use stronger and more dynamic forms of WEP.

The problem to date, however, is that these enhanced security mechanisms are proprietary, making it difficult to support multivendor client devices. As a result, the Wi-Fi Alliance took a bold step forward to expedite the availability of effective standardized wireless LAN security by defining WPA while promoting interoperability. With WPA, an environment having many different types of 802.11 radio NICs—such as public hotspots—can benefit from enhanced forms of encryption.

WPA 1.0 is a snapshot of the initial, unratified version of 802.11i, which includes Temporal Key Integrity Protocol (TKIP) and 802.1x mechanisms. The combination of these two mechanisms provides dynamic key encryption and mutual authentication, something much needed in wireless LANs.

For authentication, WPA 1.0 uses a combination of open system and 802.1x authentication. Initially, the wireless client authenticates with the access points, which authorizes the client to send frames to the access point. Next, WPA performs user-level authentication with 802.1x. During this, WPA 1.0 interfaces to an authentication server in an enterprise environment. WPA 1.0 is also capable of operating in what's known as pre-shared key mode, if no external authentication server is available, such as in homes and small offices.

The 802.11i standard is backward compatible with WPA 1.0; however, 802.11i also includes an optional Advanced Encryption Standard (AES) encryption. AES requires coprocessors not found in most access points today, which makes AES more suitable for new wireless LAN installations. The newer WPA 2.0 includes AES.

HiperLAN/2

HiperLAN/2, which stands for High Performance Radio LAN, is a wireless LAN standard developed by the Broadband Radio Access Networks (BRAN) division of the European Telecommunications Standards Institute (ETSI). HiperLAN/2 defines an efficient, high-speed wireless LAN technology that fully meets the requirements of Europe's spectrum regulations.

HiperLAN/2 has a physical layer that is similar to IEEE's 802.11a, which operates at up to 54 Mbps in the 5-GHz band using OFDM. A major difference with HiperLAN/2 is the use of a connection-oriented protocol with time division multiplexing as the basis for supporting data transfer between users. This method of transmission is efficient for multimedia applications including voice and video.

HiperLAN/2 Enhancements

The similarities between 802.11a and HiperLAN/2, however, stop at the MAC Layer. While 802.11a uses CSMA/CA to transmit packets, HiperLAN/2 uses Time Division Multiple Access (TDMA). A problem is that CSMA/CA causes stations to wait for an indefinite period of time, which is referred to as asynchronous access. With this mode of operation, there are not any regular time relationships associated with medium access. As a result, there's no guarantee of when a particular station will be able to send a packet. The lack of regular access to the medium draws down the efficiency of the system, which is not good for supporting voice and video information.

The use of TDMA in HiperLAN/2, however, offers a regular time relationship for network access. TDMA systems dynamically assign each station a time slot based on the station's need for throughput. The stations then transmit at regular intervals during their respective time slots, making more efficient use of the medium and improving support of voice and video applications.

HiperLAN/2 has a number of attractive features as compared to 802.11. The first, and probably most important, is higher throughput. Both 802.11a and HiperLAN/2 boast maximum data rates of 54 Mbps, but this doesn't represent the actual rate that information flows between the station and the access point.

The true usable maximum throughput of HiperLAN/2 is 42 Mbps, while the maximum usable throughput of 802.11a is only around 18 Mbps. This puts HiperLAN/2 well ahead of 802.11a in terms of performance of each access point.

A unique feature of HiperLAN/2 technology is the ability to interface with other high-speed networks, including 3G cellular, asynchronous transfer mode (ATM), and other Internet protocol-based networks. This can be a real advantage when integrating wireless LANs with cellular systems and WANs.

Is HiperLAN/2 a Threat to 802.11?

Despite bold predictions of mass production and deployment of HiperLAN/2 products during the second half of 2002, not many, if any HiperLAN/2 products are currently available for consumer purchase. In fact, exhaustive searches on the Internet reveal no HiperLAN/2 products available to consumers. HiperLAN/2 doesn't seem to be moving forward at any discernable pace.

Much of this has to do with regulatory issues and big supporters pulling out of the HiperLAN/2 movement. In addition, the 802.11h Task Group has been working on revisions to 802.11 that make it more suitable for deployment in Europe, which is where HiperLAN/2 could dominate if anywhere.

Essentially 802.11h is 802.11a with two additional European features. The first of these is Transmit Power Control (TPC), which enables automatic controls for keeping transmissions from interfering with other nearby systems. The second feature is Dynamic Frequency Selection (DFS), which allows the station to listen to the airspace before picking a channel. This is also an interference avoidance mechanism that the ETSI requires for operation within Europe.

802.11 currently has a definite lead in the worldwide market as the top choice for wireless LAN deployments. This makes 802.11 the only alternative for wireless LAN deployments today. Combined with the absence of HiperLAN/2 products, it's doubtful that HiperLAN/2 will catch up and become the dominant player in the wireless LAN market.

Chapter Summary

Wireless LAN components include radio NICs, access points, routers, repeaters, and antennae that enable wireless applications in buildings and campus areas. These components are building blocks for implementing wireless LANs in homes, small offices, enterprises, and public hotspots. These networks can range from having a single access point in a home or small office to hundreds of access points covering a large facility. Or, the wireless LAN might include only two users communicating directly with each other using ad hoc mode.

802.11 is by far the most prominent standard worldwide, with data rates up to 54 Mbps and operation in either the 2.4-GHz or 5-GHz frequency bands. Wi-Fi offers assurance of interoperability among manufacturers of 802.11-compliant wireless LAN components, and HiperLAN/2 is a European-based standard that is unlikely to compete heavily with 802.11.

Chapter Review Questions

You can find the answers to the following questions in Appendix A, "Answers to Chapter Review Questions."

1. Which wireless LAN component is most commonly used in home and small offices?

2. What is the primary difference between an access point and a wireless LAN router?

3. When would the use of a wireless LAN repeater make sense?

4. How does a wireless LAN radio NIC identify with which access point to associate?

5. WEP is a mandatory encryption mechanism. True or false?

6. In what frequency band does 802.11a operate in?

7. How many non-overlapping channels are available with 802.11b wireless LANs?

8. True of false: 802.11g operates at up to 54 Mbps and interoperates with 802.11b.

9. Which 802.11 frequencies are available almost worldwide?

10. What does Wi-Fi provide?

What You Will Learn

After reading this chapter, you should be able to

- ✔ Recognize specific wireless MAN applications

- ✔ Understand wireless MAN components and technologies

- ✔ Realize the different types of wireless MAN systems

CHAPTER 6

Wireless MANs: Networks for Connecting Buildings and Remote Areas

Wireless MANs satisfy needs for networking over metropolitan areas, such as cities and specific rural areas. Generally, wireless MANs provide interconnections among stationary users. In most cases, wireless MANs offer stationary outdoor connections.

Wireless MANs offer a high return on investment because companies can avoid leasing or installing expensive copper circuits or optical fiber links. In fact, it's sometimes impossible to install a wired network between two points when right-of-way restrictions prohibit the installation of wires. For example, a company might use wireless MAN components for data communications between the corporate headquarters and a nearby distribution center.

In many cases, companies can realize enough savings from a wireless MAN to pay for the equipment within one to two years. This certainly gives incentive to any company needing to establish communications between buildings spread throughout a metropolitan area.

This chapter offers examples of wireless MAN components, describes how these components interconnect to form a variety of systems, and explores the various standards.

Wireless MAN Components

Components of a wireless MAN generally come in matching pairs because they support fixed wireless connectivity from one point to another. Take a look at the primary components of a wireless MAN.

Bridges

The industry definition of a *bridge* is a device that connects two networks that might use the same or a different data-link layer protocol (Layer 2 of the OSI reference model). Figure 6-1 illustrates this concept.

Figure 6-1   Bridges Enable the Connection of Two Networks

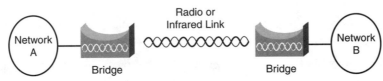

Wireless bridges are generally at each end of a point-to-point link, such as those that interconnect two buildings. A bridge has a wired port that connects to the network and a wireless port that interfaces with a transceiver. The bridge receives packets on one port and retransmits them on another port. A bridge will not start retransmission until it receives a complete packet. Because of this, stations on either side of a bridge can transmit packets simultaneously without causing collisions.

Some bridges retransmit every packet on the opposite port regardless if the packet is heading to a station located on the opposite network. A learning bridge, which is more common, examines the destination address of every packet to determine whether it should forward the packet based on a decision table that the bridge builds over time. This increases efficiency because the bridge will not retransmit a packet if it knows that the destination address is on the same side of the bridge as the sending address. Learning bridges also age address-table entries by deleting addresses that have been inactive for a specified amount of time.

The bridges within the network are transparent to users. Packets are sent through the bridge automatically. In fact, users have no idea that their packets are traversing a link leading to a different location.

Bridges Versus Access Points

Access points connect multiple users wirelessly to each other and to a wired network. For example, several users equipped with 802.11 NICs might associate with a single access point that connects to an Ethernet network. Each of these users has access to the Ethernet network and to each other. The access point in this case is similar to a bridge device, but the access point interfaces a network to multiple users. A bridge interfaces only other networks.

It's possible to use a wireless bridge indoors. For example, a wireless LAN bridge can interface an Ethernet network directly to a particular access point. This might be necessary if few devices, possibly in a far-reaching part of the facility, are interconnected through Ethernet. A wireless LAN bridge plugs into this Ethernet network and uses the 802.11 protocol to communicate with an access point that is within range. In this manner, a bridge enables the wireless connection of a cluster of users (actually a network) to an access point.

Basic Ethernet-to-Wireless Bridges

An Ethernet-to-wireless bridge (see Figure 6-2) connects directly to a single computing device through an Ethernet port and then provides a wireless connection to an access point. This makes it useful when the device, such as a printer, PC, or video game console, has an Ethernet port and no wireless NIC. In some cases, you might have no way of adding a wireless NIC, which makes a basic bridge the only way to go wireless. Printers and video game machines are common examples of this scenario.

Figure 6-2   Basic Bridge Connects a PC to a Wireless LAN

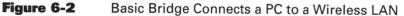
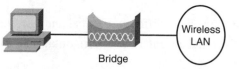

Workgroup Bridges

Workgroup bridges are the answer for connecting wireless networks to larger, wired Ethernet networks. A workgroup bridge acts as a wireless client on the wireless network, and then interfaces to a wired network. The wired side connects to an Ethernet switch that connects multiple devices. A workgroup bridge offers more robust and higher-end management and security utilities—with higher prices—as compared to a basic bridge.

Figure 6-3   Workgroup Bridge Connects to Standard Wired Networks

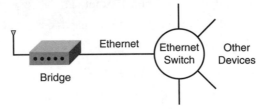

Directional Antennae

The antenna is an important element of a wireless MAN. Unlike other types of wireless networks, most antennae for wireless MANs use ***directional antennae***, mainly because they operate over wider areas. Figure 6-4 illustrates the propagation of radio waves from a directional antenna. This contrasts with an omnidirectional antenna, which transmits radio waves in all directions.

Figure 6-4   Directional Antennae Maximize the Intensity of Radio
                       Waves in One Direction

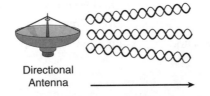

Different types of antennae have different vertical and horizontal beamwidths. For example, an omnidirectional antenna has a horizontal beamwidth of 360 degrees

and a vertical beamwidth that ranges from 7 to 80 degrees. A semidirectional antenna might have a vertical beamwidth of 20 degrees and a horizontal beamwidth of 50 degrees. Generally, the narrower the beamwidth, the longer the range when transmit power is kept constant.

Semidirectional Antennae

There are several different types of antennae that have semidirectional radiation patterns. For example, a directional patch antenna will have at least double the range as compared to an omnidirectional antenna. You can easily mount a patch antenna on a wall on one side of a facility and effectively cover a large area. A Yagi antenna, a common antenna invented by Japanese inventor Hidetsugu Yagi, is the semidirectional antenna best for long-range applications.

Semidirectional antennae effectively increase the signal's amplitude—referred to as gain—by approximately 10 times. Their use is mostly for extending wireless LANs to cover a larger area. For example, a university might employ a Yagi antenna to effectively cover a large, open, outdoor area of the campus. Wireless MANs generally span much greater distances and require greater values of gain.

Highly Directional Antennae

A highly directional antenna has an extremely narrow beamwidth, with long radiation patterns and corresponding range. To achieve this degree of directivity, you need to use dish antennae that focus the radio energy mostly in one direction. These types of antennae are expensive compared to omni- and semidirectional antennae; however, the costs may be feasible if the solution requires long range.

Many of the higher-gain directional antennae use a parabolic dish to focus the radio frequency (RF) power in one direction. A parabolic dish, for example, has a narrower horizontal and vertical beamwidth of 4 to 25 degrees. This extreme focusing of the RF power increases range significantly.

A problem, however, is that the dish antennae are subject to damage from weather because of excessive wind loading, especially if the antenna is not mounted correctly. As a result, highly directional grids that have plenty of holes in the dish are generally safer to deploy.

In addition, both semidirectional and highly directional antennae require a clear line of sight between both ends of the system. In some cases, RF signals can pass through trees and some buildings, but infrared requires an unobstructed path. RF and infrared signals also experience periodic attenuation due to obstructions moving across the path of the signal, such as passing trains and automobiles. Planning wireless MANs is difficult in city environments because of buildings that block the path between the ends of the system.

Effect of Polarization

Antenna polarization is the physical orientation of the antenna along a horizontal or vertical plane. For example, vertical polarization, which is the most common for wireless LANs, occurs when the antenna is perpendicular to the Earth. Parallel polarization applies to an antenna that is parallel to the Earth.

To maximize the transfer of RF energy from the transmitter to the receiver antenna, both antennae should have the same polarization. If one antenna has vertical polarization and the other has horizontal polarization, no transfer of power or communications will occur.

Wireless MAN Systems

Wireless MANs offer connections between buildings and users within a city or campus area through several system configurations. In most cases, the wireless MAN beams RF or infrared light from one point to another using directive antennae.

Point-to-Point Systems

A point-to-point solution uses RF or infrared signals that utilize either semidirectional or highly directional antennae to extend range across metropolitan areas, such as college campuses and cities. Range can be as high as 30 miles for RF systems using highly directional antennae. Figure 6-5 illustrates a point-to-point wireless MAN system.

Figure 6-5   Point-to-Point Wireless MAN Directly Connects Two
Points in the Network

A medical center, for example, can use a point-to-point wireless MAN to provide
a communications link between the main hospital and a remote clinic within the
same city. This resulting system, however, does not provide as much flexibility as
point-to-multipoint solutions. However, if there is a need to connect only a couple
sites, the cost of implementing a *point-to-point system* is less compared to a
point-to-multipoint system.

Point-to-Multipoint System

A typical point-to-multipoint link (see Figure 6-6) utilizes a centralized omnidirectional antenna that provides a single transceiver point for tying together multiple remote stations. For example, a building within the center of a city can host
the omnidirectional antenna, and other nearby metropolitan-area buildings can
point directional antennae at the centralized location. The central transceiver
receives and retransmits the signals.

Figure 6-6   Point-to-Multipoint Wireless MAN Interconnects Users
Through a Common, Centralized Transceiver

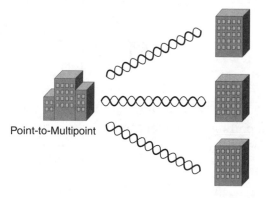

A strong advantage of the point-to-multipoint wireless MAN is that it makes the addition of new connections easy. In fact, this approach can be less expensive compared to point-to-point systems when there are multiple sites to interconnect or connect to a central location. For example, a company headquarters having many remote warehouses and manufacturing plants within the same city or rural area would benefit from a *point-to-multipoint system*.

Packet Radio Systems

A packet radio system (see Figure 6-7) utilizes special wireless routers that forward data contained within packets to the destination. Each user has a packet radio NIC that transmits data to the nearest wireless router. This router then retransmits the data to the next router. This hopping from router to router occurs until the packet reaches the destination. This mesh type networking is not new. Amateur Ham radio operators have used it for decades, and companies such as Metricom have been deploying these types of systems in cities for nearly 10 years.

Figure 6-7   Packet Radio System Hops Data Packets from the Source to Destination

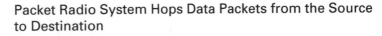

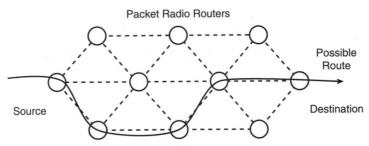

A city government might want to deploy a packet radio system to offer wireless connectivity for supporting applications through the entire city area. The installation of routers in strategic places through the city provides the necessary infrastructure. There's no need for wires for interconnecting the routers. Each router is capable of receiving and retransmitting—hopping— the packets to their destination.

This form of networking is also survivable. If one router becomes inoperative, perhaps because of a lightning strike or sabotage, adaptive routing protocols automatically update routing tables in each router so that data packets will avoid traversing the inoperative router.

Wireless MAN Technologies

Many of the wireless MAN installations utilize proprietary technologies operating in licensed bands. The licensing avoids potential RF interference by ensuring that nearby systems are using different frequencies. Even though end users follow a process of obtaining a license, it isn't time consuming because it is only done once. The problem, however, is that licensed band components are expensive.

As a result, companies prefer to utilize equipment based on standards, which generally results in fewer initial costs and lower support costs. If a manufacturer no longer supports a particular product, the company can go to a different manufacturer when modifying the network. Standards certainly improve the longevity of the system.

802.11 and Wi-Fi

Many companies deploy wireless MANs using wireless LAN standards, such as 802.11 and Wi-Fi. Chapter 5, "Wireless LANs: Networks for Buildings and Campuses," gives details on these standards. The difference is that a wireless MAN utilizes directional antennae to establish a point-to-point link between fixed points in the system. The hardware includes a wireless bridge that implements wireless LAN standards.

The use of wireless LAN hardware for metropolitan-sized networks decreases costs, but 802.11 has performance limitations when supporting larger numbers of users needing guaranteed bandwidth. In addition, RF interference is often a significant problem with 802.11 when covering large areas because of license-free operation. A competitor might install an 802.11 network that interferes with yours, and users will suffer due to sporadic performance. There is no solution because there are no legal grounds to remedy the situation.

802.16

The IEEE 802 group initiated the IEEE 802.16 working group to create standards for broadband wireless access in order to offer a high-speed, high-capacity, low-cost, scalable solution to extend fiber-optic backbones. The first IEEE *802.16* standard, published in April 2002, defines the Wireless MAN Air Interface for wireless MANs. These systems are meant to provide network access to homes, small businesses, and commercial buildings as an alternative to traditional wired connections.

With wireless base station equipment targeted at under $20,000, 802.16 can economically serve up to 60 customers with T-1 (1.5 Mbps) speed connections. That's really attractive to the typical WISP that's short on cash. In addition, 802.16 can provide a feasible backhaul for connecting wireless LAN hotspots together.

802.16 supports point-to-multipoint architecture in the 10–66 GHz range, transmitting at data rates up to 120 Mbps. At those frequencies, transmission requires line of site, and roofs provide the best mounting locations for base and subscriber stations. The base station connects to a wired backbone and can transmit wirelessly up to 30 miles to a large number of stationary subscriber stations, possibly hundreds.

To accommodate non-line-of-site access over lower frequencies for locations without line of site, IEEE published 802.16a in January 2003, which includes support for mesh architecture. 802.16a operates in the licensed and unlicensed frequencies between 2–11 GHz using Orthogonal Frequency Division Multiplexing (OFDM).

The 802.16 MAC layer supports many different physical layer specifications, both licensed and unlicensed. Through the 802.16 MAC, every base station dynamically distributes uplink and downlink bandwidth to subscriber stations using time-division multiple access (TDMA). This is a dramatic difference from the 802.11 MAC, with current implementations operating through the use of carrier sensing mechanisms that don't provide effective bandwidth control over the radio link.

The next step for the IEEE 802.16 working group is to add portability and mobility to the standard. In March 2002, the group began the 802.16e study group on Mobile Broadband Wireless Access. This group will address many different mobility issues, including providing connectivity to moving vehicles within a base station's sector.

Chapter Summary

Wireless MANs primarily use bridges with directional antennae to interconnect two or more networks over a metropolitan area. Point-to-point systems directly connect two sites; and point-to-multipoint enables multiple sites to connect through a central transceiver. Many companies utilize proprietary technologies for wireless MANs. Standards such as 802.11 and Wi-Fi enable less-expensive solutions, but potential RF interference persists. The 802.16 standard, however, promises to offer effective standards-based wireless MANs.

Chapter Review Questions

You can find the answers to the following questions in Appendix A, "Answers to Chapter Review Questions."

1. Why does a wireless MAN offer good return on investment?

2. A learning bridge forwards all packets. True or false?

3. What is the primary difference between a bridge and an access point?

4. What are examples of semidirectional antennae?

5. In regards to beamwidth, what is the primary difference between a semidirectional and highly directional antenna?

6. What is an example of a highly directional antenna?

7. What polarization would be most effective at a receiver if the transmitter were using vertical polarization?

8. What are the advantages of using point-to-multipoint systems versus point-to-point for interconnecting multiple sites?

9. What are the advantages of using packet radio for wireless MANs?

10. Which standards do wireless MANs employ?

What You Will Learn

After reading this chapter, you should be able to

- ✔ Recognize specific wireless WAN applications

- ✔ Understand wireless WAN components and standards

- ✔ Realize the various wireless WAN systems

CHAPTER 7

Wireless WANs: Networks for Worldwide Connections

Wireless WANs satisfy needs for networking over vast distances, such as countries and continents. In most cases, wireless WANs offer connections while away from the office, home, and the indoor public wireless LANs. Wireless WANs do provide coverage inside buildings, but performance in these areas is often much less than when operating outside.

The advantage of wireless WANs is wide coverage and economies-of-scale that result in low prices for subscribers. The disadvantage is that the limited availability of frequency spectrum results in low performance and limited security. Wireless WANs, however, are more practical than wireless LANs to deploy in large areas. Some performance is better than none.

For example, a wireless WAN enables someone to check her e-mail on her PDA while visiting a customer in a different city. This allows users to react quicker to situations, rather than wait to check their e-mail from the hotel room. The relatively low performance of wireless WANs adequately supports this type of application.

Wireless WANs can also provide Internet access from a stationary location. A camper, for example, can aim a satellite dish mounted on a recreational vehicle and have access to the Internet. This makes it possible to stay in touch with family, and enjoy the benefits of the web, while staying in remote areas.

This chapter offers examples of wireless WAN components, describes how these components interconnect to form a variety of systems, and explores the various technologies.

Wireless WAN Components

Wireless WANs satisfy both mobile and stationary applications. Components, therefore, vary depending on the technology and configuration of the wireless WAN. A satellite-based wireless WAN, for example, has different components than a cellular-based system.

Wireless WAN User Devices

Users of wireless WANs operate small and portable devices. This is because access to the network is available over much wider areas, and the users must carry their devices with them. For example, a business traveler can easily carry a small PDA or mobile phone and access e-mail while riding in a taxi from the airport to a hotel. Figure 7-1 illustrates the types of user devices most common to wireless WANs.

Figure 7-1   Wireless WAN User Devices Are Small for Easy Mobility

Data Collector   Mobile Phone   Laptop   Personal Digital Assistant

The use of wireless WANs to network stationary PCs is not common; however, some applications do exist. The need to set up a portable point-of-sale (POS) register at a remote area, such as a makeshift concert site, could prompt the use of a wireless WAN. A vendor selling t-shirts can process credit cards over the wireless WAN to an Internet-based processing center.

Radio NICs

Some mobile phones have integrated wireless WAN radios. Telecommunication companies, such as Verizon and Sprint, offer wireless WAN connections with voice services. The problem, however, is that several different types of wireless WANs exist, making it a challenge for users to find a mobile phone that interfaces with the type of wireless WAN they want to use.

To interface a laptop or PDA to a wireless WAN, you need to purchase an applicable wireless WAN radio NIC. Figure 7-2 shows a radio NIC available for wireless WANs. These cards can look like ones for wireless PANs and LANs; however, the card might contain one of several incompatible technologies.

Figure 7-2   Wireless Radio NICs Exist for Laptops and PDAs

Along with the purchase of hardware, the vendor generally sells access to the service that the card is designed to interface with. Telecommunications companies spend significant amounts of money to secure frequency spectrum and install hardware over vast areas. As a result, all wireless WAN providers charge for the service. This is different than wireless LAN hotspots, where many hotels and airports are finding it advantageous to offer free Internet access to wireless LAN users. This is made possible because wireless LAN deployment doesn't require much capital.

note

Be certain to purchase a wireless WAN radio NIC that interfaces with a type of wireless WAN that's available in the areas you need. Consider the coverage area, just as you would with a mobile phone, before deciding on which NIC and service to use.

In the case of using a satellite-based wireless WAN, the purchase of satellite terminal hardware becomes necessary. Mobile versions of satellite terminals have a small-parabolic (dish) reflector antenna and electronics that can fit within a medium-sized briefcase. This type of wireless WAN interface is relatively expensive. Satellite terminals are also available for more permanent installations, such as home or recreational vehicles.

Base Stations

Base stations for wireless WANs typically appear outdoors. In fact, the familiar cell towers shown in Figure 7-3 are seen scattered around cities and country areas. Similar to wireless LANs, these base stations rely on wires to connect to a distribution system that provides switching and an interface to the Internet. In most cases, the towers reside outdoors to provide maximum coverage. However, some large public facilities—such as shopping malls and airports— install cellular base stations indoors to handle larger numbers of subscribers.

Another form of wireless WAN base station is a *satellite* in orbit, which is actually a repeater in the sky. On the ground, a user aims a dish antenna at the satellite, and the satellite receives the signal and retransmits the signal back to an Earth station. (See Figure 7-4.) A strong advantage of this approach is that less infrastructure is necessary on the ground. The problem, however, is that operators must spend millions of dollars to establish a satellite system for computer traffic. This equates to expensive service charges for users.

Figure 7-3   Cell Towers Are Common Wireless WAN Base Stations

Figure 7-4   Satellites Have Signal Transponders That Send and Receive RF Signals and Solar Cells That Provide Electricity

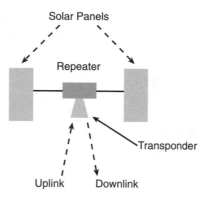

Antennae

Wireless WAN base stations and user devices use a variety of antennae depending on the type of wireless LAN. For cellular systems, the antenna on the user device is generally omnidirectional. Cell towers generally have multiple directional antennae, however, that cover vast distances.

A satellite user has a dish antenna with characteristics as shown in Figure 7-5. The transceiver, located at the focal point, transmits and receives the radio frequency (RF) signal. For example, the RF signal leaves the transmitter side of the transceiver, and the shape of the dish focuses the RF signals in one direction.

Figure 7-5   Dish antennae Have Parabolic Reflectors That Focus the Signal Power in a Beneficial Way

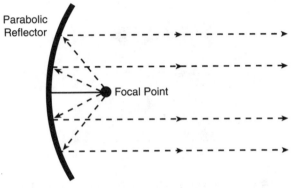

No matter how the RF signal hits the dish, the signals leave the dish in the same direction because of its parabolic shape. In fact, the opposite is also true. When the dish receives RF signals, the shape of the dish focuses the RF signals at the receiver, which is at the focal point.

note
A snow sled disk is the shape of a parabolic reflector.

Wireless WAN Systems

Most wireless WANs are cellular based, but some make use of space. Take a closer look at both of these.

Cellular-Based Wireless WANs

As shown in Figure 7-6, a cellular system consists of cell towers, concentrators, voice switches, and data gateways. The cell tower receives signals from user devices and transmits information back to the user. The voice switch connects the user device to another wireless, or wired, user through the telephone distribution system. This part of the system supports customary phones calls between users.

Figure 7-6   Cellular Systems Include Data Gateways to Augment Traditional Voice Services with Wireless Network Connections

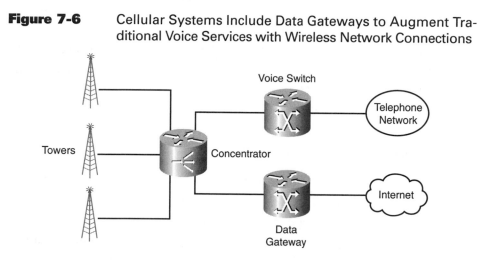

The component that makes the system a wireless WAN is the data gateway. In this case, the gateway is able to interface with data protocols in a way that makes it possible for users to surf the Internet, send and receive e-mails, and utilize corporate applications.

Text messaging is a popular application of cellular-based wireless WANs. Users converse by typing in short text messages and sending them to other users, similar to instant-messenger applications available for PCs. With smaller wireless WAN devices, however, it's important that users can save canned messages such as, "I'm traveling today and I'll call you later," which can be sent at the press of single button. Some wireless WAN devices also capture digital pictures and video that is sent across the network.

First-Generation Cellular

When mobile phones first became available, wireless communications used only analog signals. This initial cell phone system is known as first-generation cellular (*1G cellular*). When someone speaks through a 1G system, his voice is sent using frequency modulation (FM), which merely changes the frequency of carrier wave according to the audio signal. 1G systems make use of a limited number of channels that use FSK to send control signals necessary to set up and maintain the calls.

1G systems work well for voice phone calls, despite occasional crackles and pops, but they are not sufficient for sending computer data. As with the voice, analog signals must represent data. Users must interface PCs to the cellular system using a modem that converts the digital signals from the computing device into an analog form (such as FSK or PSK) that is suitable for transmission through a small, 4-KHz voice channel. This results in slow 20- to 30-kbps data rates.

1G systems also lack capacity to support an authentication and encryption mechanism. The digital FSK control channel only has enough capacity to support telephone calls. There is not enough room for sending usernames and passwords to an authentication service or coordinating encryption processes. It's quite apparent that 1G cellular was designed to carry voice, not data.

1G systems at one time covered most of the U.S. Today, however, they exist only in areas having low population density, where it's not feasible to upgrade the infrastructure to newer digital systems.

Second-Generation Cellular

Not too long ago, digital cellular became available, allowing both the voice and control channels to make use of digital signing. The first phase of this totally digital system is referred to as second-generation cellular (*2G cellular*). Most of the telecommunications operators today have 2G systems, with various enhancements occurring periodically.

The use of digital signaling for the voice channels allows for more efficient modulation. This makes it possible to support more phone calls and data over a lower frequency spectrum. In fact, 2G systems enable enhanced services—such as short messaging, authentication, and phone software updates—to be accessed wirelessly.

Enhanced versions of 2G systems (sometimes referred to as 2.5G) include even better modulation, which increases data rates and spectrum efficiency. For example, the General Packet Radio Service (GPRS) offers high-speed data rates over a global system for mobile communications (GSM) network. Maximum data rates over GPRS are 171.2 kbps. The use of GPRS, however, requires a specialized mobile phone. Also, the Enhanced Data Rate for Global Evolution (EDGE) enhances GSM using 8-level PSK, where each transmitted symbol represents 3 data bits. This results in a maximum data rate of 474 kbps.

Third-Generation Cellular

Many of the telecommunications operators are now beginning to offer what's known as third-generation cellular (*3G cellular*), with even better support for data communications. The Universal Mobile Telecommunications System (UMTS) is capable of 2-Mbps data rates for in-building implementations, up to 384 kbps in urban areas, and 144 kbps in rural areas. As a result, 3G is able to support multimedia applications.

There has been considerable argument in the wireless industry on whether 3G will replace 802.11 (Wi-Fi) wireless LAN technology. With higher data rates for indoor use, 3G is an alternative to wireless LANs. 802.11 continues, however, to have performance upgrades that significantly exceed 3G. For example, the 802.11a standard specifies data rates of 54 Mbps, which is much higher than 3G. Also, wireless LANs are much less expensive to deploy.

Wireless LANs, however, are not practical for providing coverage over wide areas. There would be too much infrastructure. 3G makes use of existing cell tower sites and distribution systems. Expenses of modifying 1G and 2G cellular systems to 3G are still high, but it's the most feasible method for providing wireless networking over wide areas.

Thus, both 3G and wireless LAN systems complement each other. This has prompted standards groups and manufacturers to find ways to seamlessly integrate 3G and wireless LANs. In fact, mobile phones and PDAs are available today that implement both technologies. With this capability, a user can roam outside the range of a wireless LAN and automatically associate with a cellular system. The problem is that standards that define this form of roaming are not yet available, which requires the user to carefully choose service providers that support the phone or PDA of choice.

Short Message Service (SMS) Applications

One of the most common services for wireless WANs is short message service (SMS), which is a text messaging system capable of sending a couple hundred characters at a time. SMS is a wireless form of the familiar instant messaging that is available from many of the ISPs. The following are additional applications of SMS for use with wireless WANs:

- **Content delivery**—SMS enables the efficient delivery of updates for user devices. For example, a user can download new ring tones and fancy backgrounds to her phone over SMS. In addition, SMS makes it possible for users to query databases and news feeds. For example, you can keep up with the latest breaking news by receiving instant updates through SMS.

- **Alerts**—Most operators offer a variety of alerts, such as voicemail waiting, sports scores, current stock prices, and other reminders. This allows you to receive updates when something that you define as important occurs.

- **Interaction**—Some television shows allow interactivity among viewers and hosts through SMS. This enables participation of the audience, which dramatically increases the viewing audience size

- **Application integration**—It's feasible for developers to integrate SMS into many corporate applications. For example, a company can have a sales management system that enables sales representatives to track customers and products. A company can usually easily add SMS to these applications. For example, the addition of an alert mechanism would be beneficial. Sales representatives would be notified that a product has gone on sale.

Many web sites use Wireless Markup Language (WML) to transform regular web pages into a format that is more easily read on a small device, such as a PDA or cell phone. WML also reduces the graphics on the page to compensate for the slower data rates of wireless WAN technologies.

note

For more information on instant messaging applications, check out the Instant Messaging Planet at http://www.instantmessagingplanet.com.

Space-Based Wireless WANs

In addition to the land-based cellular systems, the use of space-based systems provides a means for networking users over wide areas.

Satellites

The use of satellites for broadcasting television and other communications has been around for several decades. Not until recently, however, did satellite systems provide users with connections to the Internet. (See Figure 7-7.) Data rates are appreciable, with up to 1.5-Mbps downloads.

Some satellite systems support two-way exchange of data, allowing a user to send data up to the satellite (and vice versa). For example, a user's mobile device can transmit a web page request up to the satellite, and the satellite retransmits it down to the appropriate Earth station. The Earth station then sends the web page through the satellite and back down to the user. Other satellite systems, however, only support a downlink. A user's device must request the web page through another network, such as a telephone link, and the satellite broadcasts the page to the user.

Figure 7-7   Satellite System Dramatically Extends the Coverage of a Wireless WAN

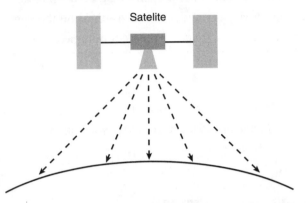

By incorporating active radio repeaters in man-made, Earth-orbiting satellites, it is possible to provide broadcast and point-to-point communications over large areas of the Earth's surface. The broadcast capability of the satellite repeater is unique and, by suitable selection of satellite antenna patterns, it can be arranged to cover a well-defined area.

Satellites are located at various points in the geostationary orbit depending on the system mission requirement. To obtain global coverage, a minimum of three satellites is required. To obtain reasonably constant RF signal levels, however, four satellites are employed. This also provides some freedom in positioning.

With satellite communications, favorable frequencies are used: power efficiency, minimal propagation distortions, and minimal susceptibility to noise and interference. Unfortunately, terrestrial systems tend to favor these frequencies as well. Space is an international domain, and the International Telecommunications Union (ITU) controls satellite frequencies.

The band of frequencies between 450 MHz and 20 GHz is the most suitable for an Earth-space-Earth radio link. It is not practical to establish links to an Earth terminal located in a climatic region of heavy rainfall at frequencies higher than 20 GHz if consistent availability is expected.

For all operating bands, the lowest-frequency spectrum is used for the downlink because it has the most severe power constraints. Lower frequencies are less sensitive to free-space attenuation when compared to the higher-uplink frequencies. Losses are easier to overcome in the uplink with the higher transmit power available at the Earth station.

The satellite acts as a signal repeater. Signals sent to it on the uplink are rebroadcast back to Earth on the downlink. The device that handles this action is referred as a transponder. The satellite transponder is analogous to a repeater in a terrestrial communications link; it must receive, amplify, and retransmit signals from Earth terminals. A satellite transponder is capable of acting as a transponder for one or more RF communications links.

Low-altitude satellites, which can have circular, polar, or inclined orbits, have orbital periods of fewer than 24 hours. Therefore, they appear to move when seen from the Earth's surface. These orbits are useful for surveillance purposes, and can be used to provide communications at extreme north and south latitudes.

One type of special interest to public data communications is the geostationary orbit. A satellite in such an orbit has a 24-hour period at an altitude of 22,300 miles and remains over a fixed location on the equator. As a result, the satellite appears motionless to an observer on Earth.

Actually, the satellite does not remain truly fixed. Even if the orbit were perfectly circular and at precisely the right altitude, natural phenomena (because of low-level lunar and planetary-gravitational fields and solar-radiation pressure) introduce slight drifts in the orbit. This slow and minor drift is corrected from time-to-time by small onboard thrusters activated by ground stations.

Because of the long RF path involved (approximately 22,300 statute miles from an Earth terminal to a satellite in geostationary orbit), a transmission delay of approximately 100 ms is experienced between an Earth terminal and the satellite. This results in an approximate Earth-to-Earth-delay of 200 ms. This causes the system to be inefficient for use with protocols, such as 802.11, that require a response after each packet of information is transmitted before transmitting the next packet. In fact, most networking protocols do not work efficiently over satellite links because the protocols expect timely acknowledgments from the destination.

Meteor Burst Communications

Billions of tiny microscopic meteors enter the Earth's atmosphere. In fact, meteors fall often throughout the day over all parts of the world. As these meteors penetrate the atmosphere, at a high altitude, they ionize into a gas. This gas is seen as a shooting star, which is an uncommon and large meteor as compared to most others.

Known as a poor man's satellite system, meteor burst communications (see Figure 7-8) bounce RF signals off meteor trails. This enables a long-haul (1,500 mile) wireless-data transmission link without the expense of launching and maintaining a satellite.

Figure 7-8   Meteor Burst Systems Use Meteor Trails to Reflect Signals Back to Earth

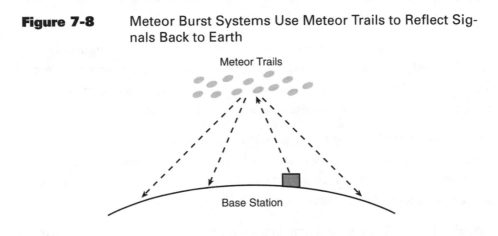

Meteor burst communications direct a 40 to 50 MHz radio wave— modulated with a data signal— at the ionized gas. The radio signal then reflects off the gas and is directed back to Earth. The availability of meteor trails is good but they are present only often enough to rely on 300 to 2400 bps. This is extremely slow, even compared to telephone modems.

However, the cost of deploying meteor burst equipment is so low compared to satellite systems that low-performance applications, such as telemetry, are feasible. Meteor burst, for example, works well for transmitting snow levels from remote mountainous areas to monitoring centers.

Wireless WAN Technologies

Wireless WANs make use of technologies that focus on modulation of voice and data. As discussed in Chapter 2, "Wireless System Architecture: How Wireless Works," modulation converts digital signals that represent information inside a computer into either RF or light signals. Wireless WANs exclusively use RF signals designed to accommodate many users. Each user has a dedicated channel, and this is different from wireless LANs, where all users share one channel. This significantly reduces interference between wireless WAN user devices and base stations.

Take a closer look at the different modulation techniques.

Frequency Division Multiple Access

Frequency division multiple access (FDMA) divides a wide-frequency band into smaller subbands, where each user transmits voice and data over their assigned subband. All users transmit their signals simultaneously. Figure 7-9 illustrates this concept. Traditional 1G cellular systems use FDMA for sending data.

Figure 7-9   FDMA Allows Simultaneous Transmissions Because Users Do Not Operate in the Same Part of the Frequency Spectrum

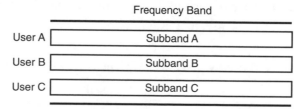

Time Division Multiple Access

As shown in Figure 7-10, *time division multiple access (TDMA)* keeps users separate by allowing only one user to transmit at any give time. Each user has an assigned time slot for transmission. Some of the older telecommunications operators utilize TDMA to offer voice and data connections over wireless WANs. For example, T1 circuits make use of TDMA for combining separate user connections over the same circuit.

Figure 7-10   TDMA Makes Users Transmit Only During Their Assigned Time Slot

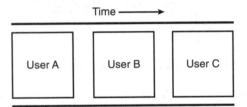

Code Division Multiple Access

Similar to FDMA, *code division multiple access (CDMA)* allows simultaneous transmissions. (See Figure 7-11.) The difference, however, is that CDMA users can occupy the entire frequency band at the same time. The users do not experience any interference, because each user modulates her signals using a different code. An advantage of CDMA is that user devices can connect to multiple base stations because of separate codes. This increases performance and reliability. Cellular systems predominately make use of CDMA wireless networks.

Figure 7-11   CDMA Assigns a Code to Each User, Which Makes It Possible for Users to Transmit Simultaneously Without Interference

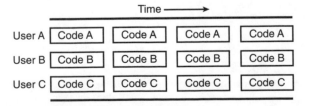

Spatial Division Multiple Access (SDMA)

SDMA accommodates multiple users by focusing a beam for each user. This is common in satellite systems. Some SDMA systems are adaptive, where the radio beams follow movement of the user. Other systems require the user device to re-associate with the next beam as users move.

note
Some wireless WAN devices, such as mobile phones, have multiple modes or bands and support more than one technology. For example, a single mobile phone can support both TDMA and CDMA. The phone automatically switches from one technology to the other depending on which network is available.

Chapter Summary

Wireless WANs include cellular towers, parabolic antennae, satellites, and telecommunications infrastructure. Most wireless WAN applications make use of outdoor connections, but some indoor facilities, such as airports and convention centers, deploy wireless WANs when large numbers of subscribers are present. Wireless WAN infrastructure is expensive compared to other types of wireless networks, but wireless WANs are the most feasible for covering countries and continents. Cellular and satellite systems are the most common forms of wireless WANs capable of providing moderate performance. Meteor burst communications is less expensive, but offers only low performance.

Chapter Review Questions

You can find the answers to the following questions in Appendix A, "Answers to Chapter Review Questions."

1. What types of user devices are most common with wireless WANs?

2. Why do wireless WAN operators always charge for services?

3. Why must you be careful when selecting a wireless WAN radio NIC for your user device?

4. What is an advantage of a satellite system?

5. Which generation of cellular systems offers data rates up to 2 Mbps?

6. Which type of wireless WAN system is most common?

7. Which of the two following cellular systems offers the highest data rates: GPRS or UMTS?

8. What is the primary issue with meteor burst communications?

9. True or false: FDMA requires users to take turns transmitting signals.

10. How does CDMA keep users from interfering with each other?

What You Will Learn

After reading this chapter, you should be able to

- ✔ Understand wireless security issues

- ✔ Describe methods to counter security problems

- ✔ Understand basic encryption and authentication technologies and standards

CHAPTER 8

Wireless Network Security: Protecting Information Resources

Security is vitally important for wireless networks, primarily because the communications signals are openly available as they propagate through the air. Companies and individuals using wireless networks must be aware of the potential issues and applicable countermeasures. This chapter discusses security threats and ways to tighten the security of a wireless network through the use of *encryption* and *authentication*.

Security Threats

As show in Figure 8-1, there are several forms of security threats to wireless networks. For example, *hackers* can steal information from a company, obtain unauthorized access to applications, and even disrupt operation of the network.

Figure 8-1   Threats to Wireless Network Security Include Passive Monitoring, Unauthorized Access, and Denial of Service (DoS)

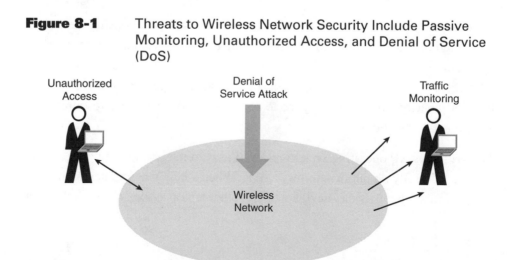

Unauthorized Access

Denial of Service Attack

Traffic Monitoring

Wireless Network

Traffic Monitoring

An experienced hacker, or even casual *snooper,* can easily monitor unprotected wireless data packets using tools such as AirMagnet and AiroPeek, which fully disclose the contents of wireless data packets. For example, snoopers can monitor all transactions occurring over the wireless portion of the network several hundred feet away from the building that has the wireless LAN. Of course, the issue is that anyone can identify usernames, passwords, credit card numbers, and so on. In fact, war drivers even post their finds on web sites, just for fun.

The solution to this problem is to, at a minimum, employ encryption between the wireless client device and the base station. Encryption alters data bits using a secret key. Because the key is secret, a hacker is not able to decipher the data. As a result, the use of effective encryption mechanisms upholds the privacy of data.

Unauthorized Access

Similar to monitoring a wireless application, someone can effortlessly access a corporate wireless network from outside the facility if the proper precautions are not taken. Someone can, for example, sit in a parked car and associate with one of the wireless base stations located inside a building. Without proper security, this person can access servers and applications residing on the corporate network. This is similar to letting a stranger inside your home or office.

Unfortunately, many companies deploy their wireless networks using the default, unsecured base station configurations, making it possible for anyone to interface with their application servers. In fact, you can go war driving and discover that 30 percent of the wireless LAN access points in an average city do not deploy any form of security. This allows anyone to access hard drives and use resources such as Internet connections.

The Windows XP operating system makes it easy to interface with wireless networks, especially on public wireless LANs. When a laptop associates with the wireless LAN, the user can navigate to any other laptop associated with the same wireless LAN. Without personal *firewall* protection, someone can browse through your hard drive. This is a tremendous security risk.

Even if you implement all security controls on access points, the possible connection of a ***rogue access point*** is a significant threat. (See Figure 8-2.) A rogue access point is an unauthorized access point on the network. An employee might purchase an access point and install it within his office without knowing the security implications. A hacker could also plant a rogue access point within a facility by purposely connecting an unprotected access point to the corporate network.

Figure 8-2   Rogue Access Points Offer an Open Port for Hackers to Exploit

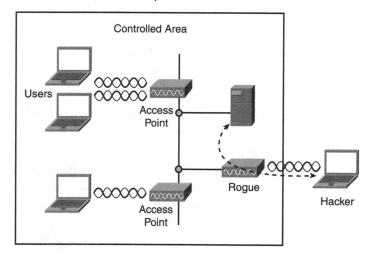

A rogue access point can be exploited because it probably won't have any encryption activated, which provides an open door for someone to easily access the corporate network from outside the facility. For that reason, a company should continually monitor for the presence of rogue access points. Keep in mind that this is a problem whether a wireless network is in place or not. Someone could connect a rogue access point to a completely wired Ethernet network.

To counter unauthorized access, the wireless network should deploy mutual authentication between client devices and the access points. Authentication is the action of proving the identity of a person or device. The wireless network should implement methods for client devices to prove identity to base stations and vice versa. This ensures the validity of the user and proves that the user is connecting to a legitimate access point. In addition, access points should authenticate with the switches to disallow the successful connection of a rogue access point.

Man-in-the-Middle Attacks

The use of encryption and authentication techniques improves the security of a wireless network; however, smart hackers can still find vulnerabilities because of the way that networking protocols operate. A definite weakness is a man-in-the-middle attack, which is when a hacker places a fictitious device between the users and the wireless network. (See Figure 8-3.) For example, a common man-in-the-middle attack exploits the common address resolution protocol (ARP) that all TCP/IP networks utilize. A hacker with the right tools can exploit ARP and take control of the wireless network.

Figure 8-3   Intermediate Devices Enable Man-in-the-Middle Attacks

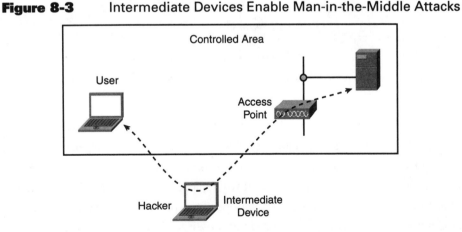

ARP is a crucial function used by sending a wireless or wired NIC to discover the physical address of a destination NIC. The physical address of a card is the same as the medium-access control (MAC) address, which is embedded in the card by the manufacturer and unique from any other NIC or network component. The MAC address is analogous to the street address of your home. Just as someone must know this address to send you a letter, a sending NIC must know the MAC address of the destination. The NIC only understands and responds to the physical MAC address.

The application software that needs to send the data will have the destination IP address, but the sending NIC must use ARP to discover the corresponding physical address. It gets the address by broadcasting an ARP request packet that announces the destination NIC's IP address. All stations will hear this request, and the station with the corresponding IP address will return an ARP response packet containing its MAC address and IP address.

The sending station will then include this MAC address as the destination address in the frame being sent. The sending station also stores the corresponding IP address and MAC address mapping in a table for a specified period of time (or until the station receives another ARP response from the station having that IP address).

A problem with ARP is that it introduces a security risk resulting from ARP spoofing. For example, a hacker can fool a station by sending, from a rogue network device, a fictitious ARP response that includes the IP address of a legitimate network device and the MAC address of the rogue device. This causes all legitimate stations on the network to automatically update their ARP tables with the false mapping.

Of course, these stations will then send future packets to the rogue device rather than to the legitimate access point or router. This is a classic man-in-the-middle attack, which enables a hacker to manipulate user sessions. As a result, the hacker can obtain passwords, capture sensitive data, and even interface with corporate servers as if they were the legitimate user.

In order to circumvent man-in-the-middle attacks using ARP spoofing, vendors such as OptimumPath implement secure ARP (SARP). This enhancement to ARP provides a special secure tunnel between each client and the wireless access point or router, which ignores any ARP responses not associated with the clients on the other end of the tunnel. Therefore, only legitimate ARP responses provide the basis for updating ARP tables. The stations implementing SARP are free from spoofing.

The use of SARP, however, requires the installation of special software on each client. Consequently, SARP is not practical for public hotspots. Enterprises, though, can install SARP on clients and be much freer from man-in-the-middle attacks.

Denial of Service

A Denial of Service (DoS) attack is an assault that can cripple or disable a wireless network. The possibility of such an attack is something that anyone deploying wireless networks should consider. Be sure to think about what could happen if the wireless network becomes unavailable for an indefinite period of time.

The severity of the DoS attack depends on the impact of the wireless network becoming inoperative. For example, a hacker could disable someone's home wireless LAN, but the result will probably just inconvenience the homeowner. A DoS attack that shuts down a wireless inventory system, however, could cause major financial loss.

One form of DoS attack is the brute-force method. For example, a huge flood of packets that uses all of the network's resources and forces the network to shut down is a DoS brute-force attack. There are tools on the Internet that enable hackers to cause excessive flooding on wireless networks. A hacker can perform a packet-based brute-force DoS attack by sending useless packets to the server from other computers on the network. This adds significant overhead on the network and takes away usable bandwidth from legitimate users.

Another way of stopping most wireless networks, especially those that use *carrier sense access*, is using a strong radio signal to dominate the airwaves and render access points and radio cards useless. Protocols such as 802.11 are very polite and let the DoS attack signal have access to the medium for as long as it wants.

The use of strong radio signals to disrupt the network is a rather risky attack for a hacker to attempt, however. Because a powerful transmitter at a close range must execute this type of attack, the owners of the wireless network can find the hacker through the use of homing tools available in network analyzers. Once the jamming source is found, authorities can stop it and possibly apprehend the culprits.

Sometimes a DoS occurrence on a wireless network is unintentional. For example, 802.11b operates in a crowded radio spectrum. Other devices such as cordless phones, microwaves, and Bluetooth can cause a significant reduction in 802.11b performance. The interference can keep a wireless network from operating.

In addition, some security mechanisms are prime targets for DoS attacks. Wi-Fi Protected Access (WPA), for example, is vulnerable to a type of DoS attack. WPA uses mathematical algorithms to authenticate users to the network. If a user is trying to get in and sends two packets of unauthorized data within one second, WPA will assume it is under attack and shut down.

The only completely effective way to counter DoS attacks is to isolate your computer in a room with heavy security and unplug it from all networks, including the Internet. This means not using a wireless network, of course. The U.S. government uses this method to protect their most sensitive data, but this solution is not practical for any enterprise or home application, where there are benefits for deploying wireless networks.

The most fundamental defense against DoS is developing and maintaining strong security practices. Actions such as implementing and updating firewalls, maintaining updated virus protection, installing up-to-date security patches, ensuring strong passwords, and turning off network devices when they are not needed should be routine practices for all companies and homeowners.

You can protect a wireless LAN against DoS attacks by making the building as resistant as possible to radio signals coming in. Here are some steps to help reduce radio signal leakage:

- If interior walls use metal studs, make sure they are grounded.
- Install thermally insulated copper or metallic film-based windows.

- Use metallic window tint instead of blinds or curtains.

- Use metallic-based paint on the interior or exterior walls.

- Run tests to determine how far the signal actually leaks outside of the build-ing. Adjust transmitter power accordingly until the leakage is eliminated or reduced to the point that it would be easy to locate a hacker.

- Aim directive access point antennas toward the inside of the building.

Because there's no way of completely countering all types of DoS attacks, con-sider a plan B if a DoS attack will cause significant damage. For example, have a process for switching to batch processing or paper-based methods if the applica-tion is subjected to a severe DoS attack. You certainly don't want potential weak-nesses in the wireless network to bring down your company!

Encryption

Encryption alters the bits of each data packet to guard eavesdroppers from decod-ing data, such as credit card numbers. Before encryption the data is called plain-text, which is easy to decode by using sniffing tools. The encryption converts the plaintext into ciphertext, which someone can decode only through the use of a proper secret key.

Many encryption methods, such as the 802.11 *Wired Equivalent Privacy (WEP)*, are symmetric—that is, the same key that does the encryption is also the one that performs the decryption. Figure 8-4 illustrates this process.

Figure 8-4   Symmetric Encryption Uses a Common Key

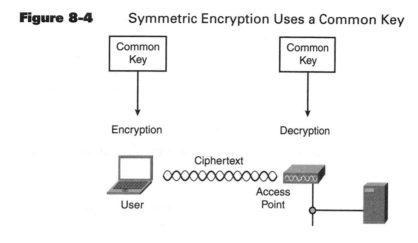

For example, the radio NIC uses key xyz to encrypt a data packet, and an access point uses key xyz to perform the decryption. This requires both the sending and receiving stations to trust each other, as is the case with a private wireless network application such as an enterprise wireless LAN. It's not practical to use symmetric keys in a public application, however, because anyone, including hackers, could obtain the key.

For symmetric encryption to be effective, the function must minimize the reuse of encryption keys by changing them often, possibly every frame transmission. This decreases the time available for a hacker to break into the network and makes it difficult—if not impossible—to compromise the security of the network. As a result, symmetric encryption mechanisms must have effective key distribution methods.

Public key cryptography uses asymmetric keys, with one that is private and another one that is public. As the name applies, the private key is secret; however, anyone can know the public key. This enables more effective encryption and authentication mechanisms because it simplifies key distribution.

An important requirement of public key encryption is that a set of public and private keys must match from a cryptographic standpoint. For example, the sending station can encrypt data using the public key, and the receiver uses the private key for decryption. The opposite is also true. The sending station can encrypt data using the private key, and the receiving station decrypts the data using the public key.

If the goal is to encrypt data, the sending station will use a public key to encrypt the data before transmission; this is shown in Figure 8-5. The receiving station uses the matching private key to decrypt the data upon reception. Each station keeps its private key hidden in order to avoid compromising encrypted information. As a result, the process allows any station to use a publicly known key to send encrypted data to any other station.

Figure 8-5 Public Key Encryption Enables All Senders of Encrypted Data to Use a Publicly Available Key

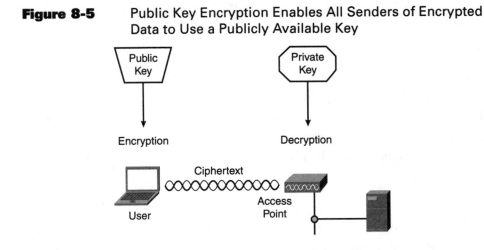

Public key cryptography works effectively for encrypting data because the public key can be made freely available to anyone wanting to send encrypted data to a particular station. A station that generates a new private key can distribute the corresponding public key over the network to everyone without worry of compromise. The public key can be posted on a website or sent unencrypted across the network.

WEP

WEP is 802.11's optional encryption and authentication standard implemented in the MAC Layer that most radio NIC and access point vendors support. When deploying a wireless network, you need to fully understand the ability of WEP to improve security.

WEP Operation

If a user activates WEP, the NIC encrypts the payload (frame body and cyclic redundancy check [CRC]) of each 802.11 frame before transmission using an RC4 stream cipher provided by RSA security. The receiving station, such as an access point or another radio NIC, performs decryption upon arrival of the frame. As a result, 802.11 WEP only encrypts data between 802.11 stations. Once the frame enters the wired side of the network, such as between access points, WEP no longer applies.

As part of the encryption process, WEP prepares a key schedule (seed) by linking the shared secret key supplied by the user of the sending station with a randomly generated 24-bit initialization vector (IV). The IV lengthens the life of the secret key because the station can change the IV for each frame transmission. WEP inputs the resulting seed into a pseudo-random number generator that produces a key stream equal to the length of the frame's payload plus a 32-bit integrity check value (ICV).

The ICV is a checksum that the receiving station recalculates and compares to the one sent by the sending station. It determines whether the transmitted data underwent any form of tampering while in transit. If the receiving station calculates an ICV that doesn't match the one found in the frame, the receiving station can reject the frame or flag the user.

WEP specifies a shared secret key to encrypt and decrypt the data. With WEP, the receiving station must use the same key for decryption. Each radio NIC and access point, therefore, must be manually configured with the same key.

Before transmission takes place, WEP combines the key stream with the payload/ICV through a bitwise XOR process, which produces ciphertext (encrypted data). WEP includes the IV in the clear (unencrypted) within the first few bytes of the frame body. The receiving station uses this IV along with the shared secret key supplied by the receiving station user to decrypt the payload portion of the frame body.

In most cases, the sending station will use a different IV for each frame (this is not required by the 802.11 standard). When transmitting messages having a common beginning, such as the sender's address in an e-mail, the beginning of each encrypted payload will be equivalent when using the same key. After encrypting the data, the beginnings of these frames would be the same, offering a pattern that can aid hackers in cracking the encryption algorithm. Since the IV is different for most frames, WEP guards against this type of attack. The frequent changing of IVs also improves the ability of WEP to safeguard against someone compromising the data.

WEP Issues

WEP is vulnerable because of relatively short IVs and keys that remain static. The issues with WEP don't really have much to do with the RC4 encryption algorithm. With only 24 bits, WEP eventually uses the same IV for different data packets. For a large, busy network, this reoccurrence of IVs can happen within an hour or so.

This results in the transmission of frames having key streams that are too similar. If a hacker collects enough frames based on the same IV, the individual can determine the shared values among them—that is, the key stream or the shared secret key. This, of course, leads to the hacker decrypting any of the 802.11 frames.

The static nature of the shared secret keys emphasizes this problem. 802.11 doesn't provide any functions that support the exchange of keys among stations. As a result, system administrators and users generally use the same keys for weeks, months, and even years. This gives mischievous culprits plenty of time to monitor and hack into WEP-enabled networks.

When to Use WEP

Despite its flaws, you should enable WEP as a minimum level of security. Many people have discovered wireless networks that use protocol analyzers, such as AiroPeek and AirMagnet. Most of these people are capable of detecting wireless networks where WEP is not in use and then use a laptop to gain access to resources located on the associated network.

By activating WEP, however, you significantly minimize this from happening, especially if you have a home or small business network. WEP does a good job of keeping most people out. Beware: There are true hackers around who can exploit the weaknesses of WEP and access WEP-enabled networks, especially those with high utilization.

Temporal Key Integrity Protocol

The 802.11i standard includes improvements to wireless LAN security. One of the upgrades is the Temporal Key Integrity Protocol (TKIP), initially referred to as WEP2. TKIP is an interim solution that fixes WEP's key reuse problem. In fact, many wireless LAN products already have TKIP as an option.

The TKIP process begins with a 128-bit temporal key shared among clients and access points. TKIP combines the temporal key with the client's MAC address and then adds a relatively large 16-octet IV to produce the key that will encrypt the data. This procedure ensures that each station uses different key streams to encrypt the data.

TKIP uses RC4 to perform the encryption, which is the same as WEP. A major difference from WEP, however, is that TKIP changes temporal keys every 10,000 packets. This provides a dynamic distribution method that significantly enhances the security of the network.

An advantage of using TKIP is that companies having existing WEP-based access points and radio NICs can upgrade to TKIP through relatively simple firmware patches. In addition, WEP-only equipment will still interoperate with TKIP-enabled devices using WEP. TKIP is a temporary solution, and most experts believe that stronger encryption is still needed.

In addition to the TKIP solution, the 802.11i standard includes the Advanced Encryption Standard (AES) protocol. AES offers much stronger encryption. AES uses the Rine Dale encryption algorithm, which is a tremendously strong encryption that replaces RC4. Most cryptographers feel that AES is uncrackable. In addition, the 802.11i standard will include AES as an option over TKIP. In fact, the U.S. Commerce Department's National Institutes of Standards and Technology (NIST) organization chose AES to replace the aging Data Encryption Standard (DES). AES is now a Federal Information Processing Standard, which defines a cryptographic algorithm for use by U.S. government organizations to protect sensitive but unclassified information. The Secretary of Commerce approved the adoption of AES as an official government standard in May 2002.

The problem with AES is that it requires more processing power than what most access points on the market today can support. As a result, the implementation of AES will require companies to upgrade their existing wireless LAN hardware to support the performance demands of AES. An issue, however, is that AES requires a coprocessor (additional hardware) to operate. This means that companies need to replace existing access points and client NICs to implement AES.

Wi-Fi Protected Access

The Wi-Fi Protocol Access (WPA) standard provided by the Wi-Fi Alliance provides an upgrade to WEP that offers dynamic key encryption and mutual authentication. Most wireless vendors now support WPA. WPA clients utilize different encryption keys that change periodically. This makes it more difficult to crack the encryption.

WPA 1.0 is actually a snapshot of the current version of 802.11i, which includes TKIP and 802.1x mechanisms. The combination of these two mechanisms provides dynamic key encryption and mutual authentication, something needed in wireless LANs. WPA 2.0 offers full compliance with the 802.11i standard.

Virtual Private Networks

If wireless users will be roaming into public areas, such as airports and hotels, strongly consider *virtual private network (VPN)* solutions. Even though VPNs are not foolproof, they provide an effective means of end-to-end encryption. VPNs are also effective when clients roam across different types of wireless networks because they operate above the dissimilar network connection levels.

Authentication

The use of mutual authentication is important in a wireless network. This will guard against many security issues, such as man-in-the-middle attacks. With mutual authentication, the wireless client and the wireless network must prove their identity to each other. This process uses an authentication server, such as Remote Authentication Dial-In User Service (RADIUS), to perform the authentication. Figure 8-6 illustrates the process of authentication.

Figure 8-6   Authentication Verifies the Identity of Users and Client Devices Through Credentials, Such as Passwords and Digital Certificates

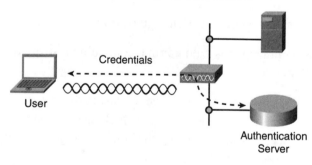

802.11 Authentication Vulnerabilities

WEP only provides a method for authenticating radio NICs to access points, not the other way around. As a result, a hacker can reroute data through an alternate unauthorized path that avoids other security mechanisms. Instead of one-way authentication, wireless networks need to implement mutual authentication to avoid this problem.

When a wireless client becomes active, it searches the medium for beacons broadcast by access points. By default, the access point broadcasts beacons containing the service set identifier (SSID) of the access point, as well as other parameters. The access point only enables association if the client SSID matches the access point SSID. This process offers a basic, but weak, form of authentication.

The major vulnerability is the fact that the SSID is sent unencrypted, which makes it visible to wireless packet sniffers. Because of this, a hacker can easily identify the SSID within the beacon frame and authenticate with the wireless network. Even if the access point is set not to broadcast the SSID—an optional feature available in only a few access points—sniffers can still obtain the SSID from association request frames sent from client devices to the access point.

802.11 offers, by default, a form of authentication called open systems authentication. In this mode, the access point grants approval for any request for authentication. The client simply sends an authentication request frame, and the access point responds with an authentication approval. This allows anyone having the correct SSID to associate with the access point.

The 802.11 standard also includes shared key authentication, an optional, more advanced form of authentication. This is a four-step process:

1. The client sends an authentication request frame.

2. The access point responds with a frame containing a string of characters called challenge text.

3. The client then encrypts the challenge text using the common WEP encryption key. The client sends the encrypted challenge text back to the access point, which decrypts the text using the common key and compares the result with the text originally sent.

4. If the decrypted text matches, the access point authenticates the client.

This seems adequate for authentication, but a problem is that shared key authentication only proves that the client has the correct WEP key.

MAC Filters

Some wireless base stations offer medium access control (MAC) filtering. When implementing MAC filtering, the access point examines the source MAC address of each incoming frame. The access point will deny frames without a MAC address that matches a specific list programmed by the administrator. As a result, MAC filtering provides a primitive form of authentication.

MAC filtering, however, has some weaknesses. For example, WEP encryption does not encrypt the MAC address field of the frame. This allows a hacker to easily sniff the transmission of frames and discover valid MAC addresses. And, a hacker can use freely available software to change the MAC address radio NICs to match a valid MAC address. This enables the hacker to masquerade as a real user and fool the access point when the legitimate user is not present on the network.

In addition, MAC filtering can be tedious to manage when there are several users. An administrator must enter each user's MAC address in a table, and then make applicable changes when new users come about. For example, an employee from another company location might need access to the wireless LAN during a visit. The administrator must determine the MAC address and program it in the system before the visitor can access the network. MAC address filtering might be adequate for smaller home and office applications, but the hands-on nature of this approach is not desirable by administrators of enterprise wireless networks.

Authentication Using Public Key Cryptography

In addition to protecting information from hackers, stations can use public key cryptography to authenticate themselves to other stations or access points. This might be necessary before an access point or controller allows a particular station to interface with a protected side of the network. Likewise, the client can authenticate the access point in a similar manner.

A station authenticates itself by encrypting a string of text within a packet using its private key. The receiving station decrypts the text with the sending station's public key. If the decrypted text matches some predetermined text, such as the station's name, the receiving station knows that the sending station is valid. The encryption of a particular string of text in this case acts as a digital signature. Figure 8-7 illustrates the concept of using public key encryption for authentication.

Figure 8-7   Public Key Encryption Enables Authentication

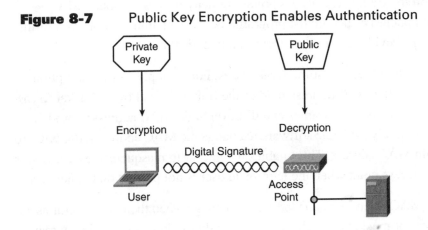

802.1x

The use of IEEE 802.1x offers an effective framework for automatically authenticating and controlling user traffic to a protected network, as well as dynamically varying encryption keys. 802.1x ties a protocol called Extensible Authentication Protocol (EAP) to both the wired and wireless network media and supports multiple authentication methods, such as token cards, Kerberos, one-time passwords, certificates, and public key authentication.

802.1x Operation

Initial 802.1x communication begins with an unauthenticated supplicant (wireless client device) attempting to connect with an authenticator (wireless base station). The base station responds by enabling a port for passing only EAP packets from the client to an authentication server located on the wired side of the base station. The base station blocks all other traffic, such as HTTP, DHCP, and POP3 packets, until the base station can verify the client's identity using an authentication server, such as RADIUS. Once authenticated, the base station opens the client's port for other types of traffic based on access rights held by the authentication server.

To get a better idea of how the 802.1x process takes place, the following specific interactions occur among the various 802.1x elements:

1. The client sends an EAP start message. This begins a series of message exchanges to authenticate the client; think of this as a group of visitors entering the front gate of a theme park and the group's leader (client) asking the gatekeeper (base station) whether they can enter.

2. The base station replies with an EAP request identity message. In the case of the theme park, the gatekeeper will ask the leader for her name and driver's license.

3. The client sends an EAP response packet containing the identity to the authentication server. The leader in this example will provide her name and driver's license, and the gatekeeper forwards this information to the group tour manager (authentication server), who determines whether the group has entry rights.

4. The authentication server uses a specific authentication algorithm to verify the client's identity. This could be through the use of digital certificates or another EAP authentication type. In this example, this process simply involves verifying the validity of the leader's driver's license and ensuring that the picture on the license matches the leader. Assume the leader is authorized.

5. The authentication server will their send an accept or reject message to the base station. In this case, an accept means the group tour manager at the theme park tells the gatekeeper to let the group enter.

6. The base station sends an EAP success packet to the client. The gatekeeper informs the leader that the group can enter the park. The gatekeeper, of course, would not let the group in if the group tour manager had rejected the group's admittance.

7. If the authentication server accepts the client, the base station will transition the client's port to an authorized state and forward additional traffic. This is similar to the gatekeeper automatically opening the gate to let in only people belonging to the group cleared for entry.

The basic 802.1x protocol provides effective authentication regardless of whether you implement 802.11 WEP keys or no encryption at all. Most major wireless network vendors, however, are offering proprietary versions of dynamic key management using 802.1x as a delivery mechanism. If configured to implement dynamic key exchange, the 802.1x authentication server can return session keys to the base station along with the accept message.

The base station uses the session keys to build, sign, and encrypt an EAP key message that is sent to the client immediately after sending the success message. The client can then use contents of the key message to define applicable encryption keys. In typical 802.1x implementations, the client can automatically change encryption keys frequently to minimize the risk of eavesdroppers having enough time to crack the key in current use.

Authentication Types

It's important to note that 802.1x doesn't provide the actual authentication mechanisms. When utilizing 802.1x, you need to choose an EAP type (such as EAP Transport Layer Security [EAP-TLS], EAP Tunneled Transport Layer Security [EAP-TTLS], or Cisco's Lightweight EAP [LEAP]), which defines how the authentication takes place. The software supporting the specific EAP type resides on the authentication server and within the operating system or application software on the client devices.

Security Policies

One of the first steps in providing wireless network security is to formulate effective policies and corresponding enforcement processes. Carefully analyze security requirements and invoke an adequate level of protection. For example, encryption should be part of all wireless network implementations. WEP might be fine for home and small office deployments, but utilize better methods— such as WPA—for corporate applications. An effective mutual authentication method, such as LEAP or EAP-TLS, is also important for corporate applications.

Assessment Steps

After deploying a wireless network, you need to implement a security assessment that ensures that the WLAN complies with security policies. For most situations, this is necessary whether the network implements effective security mechanisms. Don't put too much trust in the design of a system. It's best to run tests to be certain that the network is hardened enough to guard against unauthorized persons attacking company resources.

In fact, companies should conduct regular, periodic security reviews to ensure that changes to the wireless LAN don't make the system vulnerable to hackers. An annual review might suffice for low-risk networks; but a review each quarter or more often might be necessary if the network supports high-risk information, such as financial data, postal mail routing, and manufacturing control functions.

Review Existing Security Policies

Before getting too far with the security assessment, become familiar with company policies regarding wireless network security. This provides a benchmark for determining whether a company is complying with its own policies. In addition, you'll be able to assess and make corresponding recommendations for policy modifications. Determine whether the policy leaves any room for a disgruntled employee to access company resources.

For example, the policy should describe adequate encryption and authentication mechanisms, keeping in mind that 802.11 WEP is broken. Also, the policy should mandate that all employees coordinate with the company's IT department before purchasing or installing base stations. It's important that all base stations have configuration settings that comply with the policies and provide the proper level of security. In addition, you need to ensure that security policies are disseminated to employees in an effective manner.

Review the Existing System

Meet with IT personnel and read through related documentation to gain an understanding of the system's architecture and base stations configurations. You'll need to determine whether there are any design flaws that provide weaknesses that could allow a hacker inside the system.

Learn as much as possible about existing support tools and procedures to spot potential issues. Most companies, for example, configure the base stations over the wired Ethernet backbone. With this process, the passwords sent to open a connection with a particular base stations are sent unencrypted over the wired network. As a result, a hacker with monitoring equipment hooked to the Ethernet network can likely capture the passwords and reconfigure the base station.

Interview Users

Be sure to talk with a sample of employees to determine whether they are aware of the security policies within their control. For example, do the users know that they must coordinate the purchase and installation of wireless network components with the appropriate department? Even though the policy states this, don't count on everyone having knowledge of the policy. Someone might purchase a base station from a local office supply store and install it on the corporate network to provide wireless connectivity within the office. It's also a good idea to verify that people are using personal firewalls.

Verify Configurations of Wireless Devices

As part of the assessment, walk through the facilities with base stations and use tools to capture the base station configurations. If the company has centralized support software in place, you should be able to view the configuration settings from a single console attached to the wired side of the network. This is to determine which security mechanisms are actually in use and whether they comply with effective policies.

For example, the policies might state that base stations must disable the physical console port, but while testing you determine that most base stations have the ports enabled. This would indicate noncompliance with the policies, and it would enable a hacker to reset the base station to the factory default settings with no security enabled. In addition, look at the firmware version of each base station to see if it's up-to-date. Older firmware versions might not implement the more recent patches that fix encryption vulnerabilities.

Also, investigate base stations' physical installations. As you walk through the facilities, investigate the installation of base stations by noting their physical accessibility, antenna type and orientation, and radio wave propagation into portions of the facility that don't have physical security controls. The base stations should be mounted in a position that would make it difficult for someone to physically handle the base station and go unnoticed.

A base station simply placed on top of a bookshelf, for example, would make it easy for a hacker to swap the base station with a rogue one that doesn't have any security enabled. Or, the hacker could attach a laptop to the console port to reset the base station. If the base stations are all mounted above the ceiling tiles and out of plain view, however, someone would need to use a ladder and would probably be noticed by an employee or security guard.

Identify Rogue Base Stations

A problem that's difficult to enforce and significantly undercuts a network's security is when an employee installs a personal base station in her office. Most of the time, these installations don't comply with security policies and result in an open, unsecure entry port to the corporate network. In fact, a hacker can utilize sniffing tools to alert him when such an opportunity exists.

As a result, scan for these unauthorized base stations as part of the assessment. Most companies will be surprised to learn how many they find. The most effective method for detecting rogue base stations is to walk through the facilities with sniffing tools. In addition, the company should periodically scan the network for potential rogue base stations from the wired side of the network. This is available in many of the centralized wireless network management systems.

Perform Penetration Tests

In addition to hunting for rogue base stations, try going a step further and attempt to access corporate resources using common tools available to hackers. For example, can you utilize AirSnort to crack through WEP? Is it possible to associate with a base station from outside the company's controlled perimeter? Of course your job will be easy if WEP is turned off. If strong encryption and authentication techniques are in use, you'll likely not find a way in.

Analyze Security Gaps

The information you gather during the assessment provides a basis for understanding the security posture of a company or organization. After collecting information, spend some time thinking about potential gaps in security. This includes issues with policy, network architecture, operational support, and other items that weaken security, such as presence of unauthorized base stations and abilities to penetrate the network. This requires you to think like a hacker and uncover any and all methods that make it easier for someone to penetrate and access (or control) company resources through the wireless network.

Recommend Improvements

As you spot weaknesses, research and describe methods that will counter the issues. Start by recommending improvements to the policies, which dictate what the company requires in terms of security for the wireless networks. This provides a basis for defining technical and procedural solutions that strengthen the system's security to a level that protects the company's interests.

Common Security Policies

With any wireless network, consider policies that will protect resources from unauthorized people. Here's a look at what you should include.

Place Wireless Users Outside a Firewall

Consider implementing a wireless demilitarized zone (DMZ) by placing a firewall between the wireless network and the corporate network. (See Figure 8-8.) With this approach, equip each client device with a virtual private network (VPN) that the protected network will accept. As a result, a hacker would need to utilize a correctly configured VPN—which is difficult to do— to gain access to company resources.

Figure 8-8   Firewalls Offer Additional Security to Wireless Networks

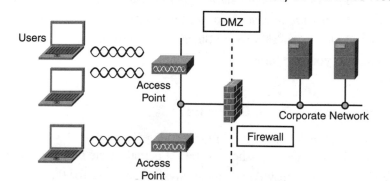

The problem with a VPN solution for all users is that it's difficult to manage and sometimes slows performance. As a result, mainly consider VPNs if users will roam into public areas.

Use Effective Encryption

Skilled hackers can crack into a WEP-protected network using freely available tools. However, WEP does a good job of protecting many home and business networks from the general public. To crack WEP, you need to know how to use complicated tools and capture a lot of network packets, something that most people won't bother with unless the network resources are extremely valuable and they have infinite patience. The use of standard 802.11 WEP for networks with low attack risk is a minimum for any security policy.

If your wireless network hardware supports a form of encryption (such as WPA) that changes keys often, use it. This offers a much more secure solution than using static methods such as WEP. If extremely high security is necessary, utilize superior standards, such as AES.

Ensure Firmware Is Up-to-Date

Vendors often implement patches to firmware in base stations and radio NICs that fix security issues. Start by upgrading the firmware in the base station soon after pulling it out of the box. Make it a habit to periodically check that all devices have the most recent firmware releases to cover up all known security holes. This is why it's a good idea to make certain you can easily upgrade the firmware in the base stations that you purchase.

Physically Secure Base Stations

Some base stations will revert to factory default settings, which do not provide any security, when someone pushes a reset. This makes the base station a fragile entry point. As a result, provide adequate physical security for the base station hardware.

For example, don't place a base station within easy reach on a table in the office. Instead, mount them out of view above ceiling tiles. Some base stations don't have reset buttons, but they allow you to reset through an RS-232 cable via a console connection. To prevent this, be sure to disable the console port.

Also, don't leave base stations within reach of a hacker who can replace a legitimate safeguarded base station with an unsecured, rogue base station that accepts access from any user. In fact, it's a good idea to conceal the base station as much as possible to make it more difficult for a hacker to find. Be sure, however, to note the location of the wireless hardware; otherwise, you'll have a difficult time finding them yourself.

Disable base stations during outage periods. If possible, shut down the base stations when users don't need them. This limits the window of opportunity. You could pull the power plug on each base station; however, consider deploying power-over-Ethernet equipment that provides this feature through centralized operational support tools.

Assign Strong Passwords to Base Stations

Don't use default passwords for base stations. Default passwords are well known, making it easy for someone to change configuration parameters on the base station to her advantage. Instead, use passwords that are difficult to guess. In fact, it's a good idea to use a mix of uppercase and lowercase letters, as well as special symbols. Be sure to alter these passwords periodically. Also, ensure that passwords are encrypted before being sent over the network.

Don't Broadcast SSIDs

If this feature is available, you can avoid having user devices automatically sniff the SSID being used by the wireless LAN access point. Windows XP and other monitoring tools will automatically sniff the 802.11 beacon frames to obtain the SSID. With SSID broadcasting turned off, the base station will not include the SSID in the beacon frame, making most sniffing tools useless. In addition, Windows and XP users will not see that the wireless LAN exists.

The disabling of SSIDs isn't foolproof, however, because someone can still monitor 802.11 association frames and recover the SSID. Shutting off the broadcast mechanism, however, will limit access.

Reduce Propagation of Radio Waves

Through the use of directional antennae, it's possible to confine the propagation of radio waves within an area where hackers are not able to physically access. For example, a wireless network design could specify antenna gain and orientation to reduce the spillage of radio waves outside the perimeter of the facility. This not only optimizes coverage, it also minimizes the ability for a snooper to eavesdrop on user signal transmissions or interface with the corporate network through an access point.

Implement Personal Firewalls

If a hacker is able to associate with a base station, the hacker can easily access files on other users' devices through the Windows operating system that are associated with an access point connected to the same wireless LAN. As a result, it's crucial that all users disable file sharing for all folders and utilize personal firewalls. This is crucial when users are operating in public locations.

Monitor Base Station Configuration

Utilize operational support tools to continually monitor the network and check for base stations that don't conform to configuration policies. A base station that doesn't match specific security settings has likely been reset or is possibly a rogue base station.

If base stations are found with improper settings, restore the settings as soon as possible. Be sure to encrypt management traffic, however, through the use of secure Simple Network Management Protocol (SNMP). SNMP Version 1, for example, sends everything in the clear. You can also deploy intrusion detection sensors, available in some operational support tools, to identify the presence of hackers based on invalid MAC addresses. The main idea is to provide alerts if suspicious behavior is occurring.

Control Deployments

Ensure that all employees and organizations within the company coordinate the installation of wireless networks with the appropriate IT group. For example, forbid the use of unauthorized access points. Mandate the use of approved vendor products after you've had a chance to verify appropriate security safeguards.

Maintain a list of authorized radio NIC and base station MAC addresses that you can use as the basis for identifying rogue base stations during surveys. In addition, deploy management tools that force base stations to comply with corporate security policies.

With these recommendations in mind, you have a basis for forming a solid security policy. When deciding on which techniques to implement, however, consider the actual security needs. For example, WEP might be good enough for home and small business wireless LANs. If you work for a financial institution or retail store transmitting sensitive data, concentrate on using something stronger, such as WPA or AES.

Chapter Summary

Security is one of the most important and complex elements of wireless networks. The ability of a hacker to monitor traffic, gain unauthorized access to valuable resources, and deny the service of a wireless network are issues that you must consider. Through the use of effective encryption and authentication, it's possible to significantly minimize threats. Keep in mind, however, that the necessary level of security depends on requirements. An acceptable level of security for a home application is much lower than what's needed for an enterprise.

Chapter Review Questions

You can find the answers to the following questions in Appendix A, "Answers to Chapter Review Questions."

1. What are the three major security threats of a wireless network?

2. What is the primary means for guarding against traffic monitoring?

3. How do you keep hackers from gaining access to company resources through the wireless network?

4. What method will help alleviate the implications of a successful DoS attack?

5. Why is WEP not acceptable for protecting sensitive information?

6. How is TKIP different than WEP?

7. WPA uses TKIP and is a subset of the 802.11i standard. True or false?

8. Why is the use of MAC address filters not effective?

9. What is a rogue access point, and why does it pose a problem?

10. What should you install on a laptop that a user will utilize on a public wireless LAN to avoid unauthorized people from accessing files on the laptop?

Answers to Chapter Review Questions

Chapter 1

1. What is a distinguishing attribute of a wireless network as compared to a general wireless communication system?

   Answer: In a wireless network, communications takes place between computer devices.

2. What types of information does a wireless network support?

   Answer: E-mails, messages, web pages, database records, streaming video, and voice.

3. What are the four types of wireless networks?

   Answer: Wireless PAN, LAN, MAN, and WAN.

4. What is the typical maximum range of a wireless PAN?

   Answer: 50 feet.

5. True or false: A wireless PAN consumes little power from small handheld computer devices.

   Answer: True.

6. What is a common standard for wireless LANs?

   Answer: IEEE 802.11 or Wi-Fi.

7. What relatively new standard applies to wireless MANs?

Answer: IEEE 802.16.

8. Why do wireless WANs not effectively satisfy requirements for indoor wireless networks?

Answer: Wireless WAN systems are generally installed outdoors, and the signals lose strength before reaching the inside of the facility.

9. What is a common application of wireless networks in homes and small offices?

Answer: Sharing Internet connections among multiple, mobile computers is a common application.

10. What are examples of applications for wireless WANs?

Answer: Access to Internet applications from outdoor locations, real-estate transactions, field-service and sales calls, vending-machine status, and utility-meter reading are a few examples.

Chapter 2

1. Which wireless NIC form factors are best for small wireless computer devices?

Answer: PC Card, Mini-PCI, and CompactFlash.

2. What are examples of elements that impair the propagation of wireless communications signals through the air medium?

Answer: Rain, snow, smog, and smoke.

3. What is the primary purpose of a base station?

Answer: Interfaces the wireless communications signals traveling through the air medium to a wired network.

4. What are common features of wireless middleware?

Answer: Optimization techniques, intelligent restarts, data bundling, screen shaping and reshaping, and end-system support.

5. On what layers of the OSI reference model do wireless networks operate?

Answer: Physical layer and data link layer.

6. How is throughput different from data rate?

Answer: Throughput doesn't include overhead of protocols.

7. A computer device stores data in analog form. True or false?

Answer: False.

8. A wireless NIC must convert the information into what type of signal before transmission through the air medium?

Answer: Analog.

9. Which medium access protocol is common with wireless networks?

Answer: CSMA.

10. Explain how the ARQ form of error control works.

Answer: The receiving wireless NIC performs error checking and sends a request to the sending wireless NIC to retransmit the frame if errors are found.

Chapter 3

1. RF signals offer relatively short range as compared to light signals. True or false?

Answer: False.

2. What type of weather impacts RF signals the most?

Answer: Heavy rain.

3. Why does interference cause errors in wireless networks?

Answer: The interference causes the receiver to misunderstand the signal because two signals are present at the same time.

4. What are sources of RF interference?

Answer: General examples include cordless phones, microwave ovens, and Bluetooth devices.

5. Multipath affects higher data rates more than lower data rates for 2.4-GHz systems. True or false?

Answer: True. The receiver has difficulties with differentiating one bit from another when demodulating high data rate signals because the bits are close together.

6. What is meant by a diffused infrared light system?

Answer: A system that emits light in all directions that reflects off of the ceiling and walls.

7. Approximately up to what range do direct infrared systems operate?

Answer: 1 mile.

8. How does modulation make it possible to transmit information through the air?

Answer: Modulation superimposes an information signal onto a carrier signal that has a frequency suitable for propagating through the air.

9. What attributes of a signal does QAM change in order to represent information?

Answer: Amplitude and phase.

10. Spread spectrum generally requires user licenses. True or false?

Answer: False.

Chapter 4

1. What form factors are common for wireless PAN radio cards?

Answer: PC Card and CF.

2. What application can strongly benefit through the use of a wireless USB adapter (also referred to as a wireless dongle)?

Answer: Any application that can benefit from interfacing with a PC or laptop through the USB port, such as PDA, wireless mouse, and wireless digital camera for synchronization purposes.

3. When would the use of a wireless PAN router make sense?

Answer: For applications limited to the size of a room, such as in homes and small offices.

4. What is the general maximum coverage area of a wireless PAN?

Answer: Within 30 feet, such as within a room.

5. Which IEEE standards group uses Bluetooth as the basis for the standard?

Answer: 802.15.

6. What frequency band does Bluetooth operate in?

Answer: 2.4 GHz.

7. What is the primary issue of using Bluetooth around 802.11 wireless LANs?

Answer: They both operate in the same 2.4 GHz frequency band, which can result in interference and degradation in performance.

8. A Bluetooth-enabled device is always transmitting. True or false?

Answer: False.

9. What is the highest possible data rate of an IrDA device?

Answer: 4 Mbps.

10. What is a benefit of IrDA as compared to Bluetooth?

Answer: IrDA is immune from RF interference with wireless LANs.

Chapter 5

1. Which wireless LAN component is most commonly used in home and small offices?

Answer: Wireless LAN router.

2. What is the primary difference between an access point and a wireless LAN router?

Answer: A wireless LAN router actually routes packets to their destination. Access points don't implement DHCP and NAT. Routers do implement DHCP and NAT.

3. When would the use of a wireless LAN repeater make sense?

Answer: When extending the range of an access point or router to an area where wires can't be run feasibly.

4. How does a wireless LAN radio NIC identify with which access point to associate?

Answer: The radio NIC listens for beacons being sent periodically by each access point and associates with the access point having the strongest beacon signal.

5. WEP is a mandatory encryption mechanism. True or false?

Answer: False.

6. What frequency band does 802.11a operate in?

Answer: 5 GHz.

7. How many non-overlapping channels are available with 802.11b wireless LANs?

Answer: Three.

8. True or false: 802.11g operates at up to 54 Mbps and interoperates with 802.11b.

   Answer: True.

9. Which 802.11 frequencies are available almost worldwide?

   Answer: 2.4 GHz (802.11b and 802.11g).

10. What does Wi-Fi provide?

    Answer: A product having Wi-Fi certification will interoperate with other products that have Wi-Fi certification, regardless of the manufacturer.

Chapter 6

1. Why does a wireless MAN offer good return on investment?

   Answer: Wireless MANs eliminate the need to install expensive cabling or lease communications circuits.

2. A learning bridge forwards all packets. True or false?

   Answer: False.

3. What is the primary difference between a bridge and an access point?

   Answer: A bridge connects networks together. An access point connects end users.

4. What are examples of semidirectional antennae?

   Answer: Patch and Yagi.

5. In regards to beamwidth, what is the primary difference between a semidirectional and highly directional antenna?

   Answer: A highly directional antenna has a much narrower beamwidth, which increases range if the power remains constant.

6. What is an example of a highly directional antenna?

Answer: Dish antenna.

7. What polarization would be most effective at a receiver if the transmitter were using vertical polarization?

Answer: Vertical polarization.

8. What are the advantages of using point-to-multipoint systems versus point-to-point for interconnecting multiple sites?

Answer: Point-to-multipoint can be less expensive and easier to add more sites.

9. What are the advantages of using packet radio for wireless MANs?

Answer: Packet radio routers don't require any cabling between them, and the system is relatively survivable because packets can take a different route if a router becomes inoperative.

10. Which standards do wireless MANs employ?

Answer: 802.11, Wi-Fi, and 802.16.

Chapter 7

1. What types of user devices are most common with wireless WANs?

Answer: Laptops, PDAs, and mobile phones.

2. Why do wireless WAN operators always charge for services?

Answer: Wireless WANs are expensive to install.

3. Why must you be careful when selecting a wireless WAN radio NIC for your user device?

Answer: There are many different types of wireless WANs that are not compatible with each other.

4. What is an advantage of a satellite system?

Answer: It can cover vast areas. A single satellite can cover roughly one-third of the Earth's surface.

5. Which generation of cellular systems offers data rates up to 2 Mbps?

Answer: Third generation (3G).

6. Which type of wireless WAN system is most common?

Answer: Cellular systems.

7. Which of the two following cellular systems offers the highest data rates: GPRS or UMTS?

Answer: UMTS.

8. What is the primary issue with meteor burst communications?

Answer: Low data rates.

9. True or false: FDMA requires users to take turns transmitting signals.

Answer: False.

10. How does CDMA keep users from interfering with each other?

Answer: Each user transmits using a different code.

Chapter 8

1. What are the three major security threats of a wireless network?

Answer: Traffic monitoring, unauthorized access, and DoS.

2. What is the primary means for guarding against traffic monitoring?

Answer: Utilize encryption.

3. How do you keep hackers from gaining access to company resources through the wireless network?

Answer: Incorporate the use of effective authentication.

4. What method will help alleviate the implications of a successful DoS attack?

Answer: Have an alternative plan to carry on business in a manner that doesn't require the use of the wireless network.

5. Why is WEP not acceptable for protecting sensitive information?

Answer: Hackers are able to crack the WEP encryption algorithm through the use of publicly available tools.

6. How is TKIP different than WEP?

Answer: TKIP make use of a dynamic key distribution mechanism that updates keys periodically, whereas WEP makes use of static keys that don't change.

7. WPA uses TKIP and is a subset of the 802.11i standard. True or false?

Answer: True.

8. Why is the use of MAC address filters not effective?

Answer: It's difficult to manage and easy to spoof.

9. What is a rogue access point, and why does it pose a problem?

Answer: A rogue access point does not have any security features set and is put in by a hacker or employee. The rogue access point offers an open port to the network for hackers to exploit.

10. What should you install on a laptop that a user will utilize on a public wireless LAN to avoid unauthorized people from accessing files on the laptop?

Answer: Personal firewall.

Glossary

1G cellular The initial (first-generation) cellular phone system that used analog signaling. This system did not effectively support the transmission computer data.

2G cellular The first cellular phone system (second-generation) that used digital signaling that supports data rates of under 20 kbps.

3G cellular A modified (third-generation) version of 2G cellular that offers better support for data communications, such as higher data rates.

802.11 A standard published by the IEEE that defines the radio characteristics and operation of a medium-range radio frequency LAN. Specifies the use of CSMA as the primary method for sharing access to a common air medium.

802.15 A standard published by the IEEE that defines the radio characteristics and operation of wireless PANs. 802.15 is based on the Bluetooth specification.

802.16 A standard published by the IEEE that defines the radio characteristics and operation of wireless MANs.

802.3 A standard published by the IEEE that defines the signal characteristics and operation of a wired local-area network. Defines the use of CSMA, which is similar to 802.11 wireless LANs.

access point A type of base station that wireless LANs use to interface wireless users to a wired network and provide roaming throughout a facility.

ad hoc mode A configuration of a wireless network that allows communications directly from one user device to another, without the need to travel through a base station. Ad hoc mode applies to both wireless PANs and wireless LANs.

analog signal A signal whose amplitude varies continuously as time progresses. A radio wave is an example of an analog signal.

antenna   A physical device that converts electrical signals to radio or light waves—and vice versa—for propagation through the air medium. Antennae may be omnidirectional, which distributes radio waves in all directions, or directional, which focus the radio waves more in one direction than others.

association   A process whereby an 802.11 station (computer device) becomes a part of the wireless LAN. After association, the user can utilize network services.

authentication   The process of proving the identity of a user or base station. The use of usernames and passwords is a common authentication method, but many other, more-sophisticated authentication mechanisms exist. For example, digital certificates can offer a means of authentication without user intervention.

base station   Hardware that interfaces wireless computing devices together and to a wired network. Access points and wireless routers are types of wireless LAN base stations.

Bluetooth   A specification published by the Bluetooth Special Interest Group that defines the radio characteristics and operation of a short-range, low-power radio frequency network. Many devices today support Bluetooth, but 802.15 is developing applicable standards.

bridge   A device that interconnects two networks at Layer 2. A bridge forwards data packets to another network based on the MAC address found in the packet header. Bridges play a key role in the deployment of wireless MANs.

carrier sense access   A process of sharing a common medium by first determining whether the medium is idle before transmitting data. This is part of the CSMA protocol.

carrier signal   The primary RF signal that carries data through the air medium. Various modulation types vary the carrier signal frequency, phase, or amplitude to represent information.

CDMA (code division multiple access)   A process where each user modulates their signals with a different, noninterfering code.

CDPD (Cellular Digital Packet Data)   A technology that enables the transmission of data over analog cell phone systems with data rates of 19.2 kbps. CDPD is becoming obsolete as newer 3G systems are becoming available.

CF (CompactFlash)   A small NIC for PDAs, cameras, and other small computer devices. Bluetooth and 802.11 CF NICs are readily available.

client device   Hardware having a user interface that enables the use of wireless network applications. Client device is another name for computer device.

computer device   Any end point of a wireless network, such as a laptop, PDA, or robot. The computer device is often referred to as a client device.

CSMA (carrier sense multiple access)   A process that allows multiple 802.11 stations to share a common air medium. Stations attempt to only transmit data when no other station is transmitting. Otherwise, collisions will occur and the station must retransmit the data.

data   Information, such as electronic files, that is stored and sent over a wireless network. Often data are sent in multiple packets, which are sent separately through the network.

data rate   The number of bits per second (bps) that data is sent. For example, 802.11b wireless LANs operate at up to 11 Mbps.

DCF (distributed coordination function)   A part of the 802.11 standard that defines how stations will contend for access to the air medium. DCF makes use of CSMA to regulate traffic on the network.

DHCP (Dynamic Host Configuration Protocol)   A protocol that automatically assigns unique IP addresses within an assigned range to network devices. Most home and public wireless LANs implement DHCP, making it easy for users to gain access to the network. DHCP automatically assigns a valid IP address to these users.

digital certificate   An electronic message that contains the credentials of a particular user. Digital certificates are used as a means for authenticating users or their computer devices.

digital signal   A signal that varies in amplitude steps as time advances. The digital signal represents data within a computer device. The digital signal must be converted to an analog form—known as modulation—before the data can be sent through the air medium.

DSSS (direct sequence spread spectrum)   A type of spread spectrum where a spreading code increases the signal rate of the data stream to diffuse the signal over a wider portion of the frequency band. 802.11b wireless LANs make use of direct sequence.

directional antenna   A type of antenna that focuses radio waves and range more in one direction than others. Directional antennae are commonly found in wireless MANs and wireless WAN systems. The directivity of the antenna increases range in one direction and decreases range in other directions.

distribution system   A wired system that physically interconnects access points in a wireless LAN. A common distribution system for wireless LANs, for example, is Ethernet.

encryption   The scrambling of data bits according to a key prior to sending the data over a network. WEP and WPA are examples of encryption that wireless LAN utilize.

Ethernet   A name that depicts 802.3 wired LANs. Ethernet is a common type of network that companies use to interconnect PCs and servers. Ethernet provides the distribution system of most wireless LANs.

FDMA (frequency division multiple access)   A process that divides a relatively wide frequency band into smaller subbands, where each user transmits voice and data over an assigned subband.

FHSS (frequency hopping spread spectrum)   A type of spread spectrum where the transceiver hops from one frequency to another, according to a known hopping pattern, to spread the signal over a wider portion of the frequency band. Older 802.11 wireless LANs utilize frequency hopping.

firewall   A device that keeps users connecting to a specific part of the network from accessing important resources. Because of their vulnerability, access points of wireless LANs are often placed outside the firewall.

frequency   The number of times per second that a signal repeats itself. Often measured in Hertz (Hz), which is the number of cycles occurring each second. Frequencies of wireless LANs, for example, are within the 2.4-GHz and 5-GHz bands.

FSK (frequency shift-keying)   A modulation process that makes slight changes to the frequency of the carrier signal to represent information in a way that's suitable for propagation through the air.

GPS (global positioning system)   A system that enables people having a GPS client device to easily determine their geographical position. GPS offers the basis of an excellent navigation system, as well as location-based services over wireless networks.

hacker A person who has the desire and ability to steal information that resides on a network. Hackers often try breaking into corporate systems for fun and to exploit the vulnerabilities of wireless networks.

hotspot The location of a public wireless LAN. Hotspots are found within areas where people congregate with computer devices including airports, hotels, convention centers, and coffee shops.

interference Unwanted signals that disrupt the operation of a wireless network. The presence of interference decreases the performance of a wireless network.

interoperability A condition where computer devices are able to successfully interface with a wireless network.

IP (Internet Protocol) A protocol that routes packets between computer devices attached to a network. The IP places a header field in front of each packet that contains the source and destination IP address of the packet.

IP address A numerical address corresponding to a connection of a network device to the network. For example, every wireless network NIC will have an IP address. Each NIC must have an IP address associated with it if the user will be making use of TCP/IP applications, such as sending and receiving e-mail, browsing the web, or interfacing with a corporate application server.

IPSec (IP Security) A protocol that supports secure exchange of packets at the network layer of a network. IPSec is commonly implemented in VPNs and encrypts data packets across the entire network; often referred to as end-to-end encryption.

IrDA (Infrared Data Association) A standard specifying an interoperable, low-cost, low-power, serial data communications standard for short-range applications. IrDA is found in many laptops and PDAs.

LDAP (Lightweight Directory Access Protocol) A protocol that enables accessing information directories.

location-based services The ability to track the location of users and deliver information to them that relates to position within a particular area.

medium access control (MAC) layer A part of a network architecture that manages and maintains communications on a shared medium. The MAC layer is the brains of a NIC or base station and enforces the rules all devices must follow.

medium   The space in which communications signals, such as radio waves, propagate. With wireless networks, the medium is air.

medium access   A process whereby multiple computer devices share a common medium. The most common medium access method for wireless networks is CSMA.

modulation   Modulation creates a radio or light signal from the network data so that it is suitable for propagation through the air medium. Examples of modulation types are FSK, PSK, and QAM.

NAT (Network Address Translation)   A protocol that maps official IP addresses to private addresses that may be in use on their internal networks. For example, a broadband Internet service provider may offer only one official IP address to a home owner. NAT, along with DHCP, enables the homeowner to have multiple PCs and laptops sharing the single official IP address.

NIC (Network Interface Card)   A hardware device that interfaces a computer device to a network. Also known as radio card and client card.

noise floor   The amplitude of electromagnetic signals in a particular area while the wireless network is not operating.

OFDM (orthogonal frequency division multiplexing)   A process that divides a modulated signal into multiple subcarriers, prior to transmission, through the air medium to improve performance. 802.11a and 802.11g wireless LANs, and some proprietary wireless MANs, utilize OFDM.

optical fiber   A long piece of small-diameter glass with a covering that carries light signals. An optical fiber cable has a protective coating, making it difficult to distinguish from copper-based cables.

PC Card   A credit-card–sized device that provides extended memory, modems, connectivity to external devices, and wireless network capabilities to small computer devices, such as laptops and PDAs. Many PC Cards implement Bluetooth and 802.11 technologies.

PDA (personal digital assistant)   A small device that people use to store contact information, schedules, and to-do lists. Some PDAs run software programs, such as e-mail clients and web browsers.

point-to-multipoint system   A system where communications is directly from one user to several others.

point-to-point system   A system where communications is directly from one user to another.

PSK (phase shift keying)   A modulation process that makes slight changes to the phase of the carrier signal in order to represent information in a way that's suitable for propagation through the air.

public wireless LAN   A type of wireless LAN, often referred to as a hotspot, that anyone having a properly configured computer device can access.

QAM (quadrature amplitude modulation)   A modulation process that makes slight changes to the amplitude and phase of the carrier signal to represent information in a way that's suitable for propagation through the air.

radio NIC   A type of NIC that transmits and receives RF signals.

RADIUS (Remote Authentication Dial-In User Service)   An authentication and accounting system that many WISPs use to handle access control and billing on wireless networks.

repeater   A device that receives and retransmits signals for the sole purpose of extending range.

RF signal   A radio frequency signal that is designed to propagate through the air medium.

rogue access point   An access point that is unauthorized and has configuration settings that might enable someone to gain access to network resources.

router   A type of base station that implements special networking protocols, such as DHCP and NAT, which enable users to use TCP/IP applications.

satellite   A signal repeater located in orbit around the Earth. Satellites offer wireless WAN coverage using radio signals.

snooper   Someone who casually—and usually inadvertently—disrupts a wireless network.

spread spectrum   The spreading of the carrier signal over a wider part of the frequency spectrum. Direct sequence and frequency hopping are two types of spread spectrum.

TCP (Transmission Control Protocol)   A protocol that establishes and maintains connections between computer devices attached to a network. TCP is used in conjunction with IP, which is commonly referred to as TCP/IP.

TDMA (time division multiple access) A process that allows only one user to transmit in any given time slot. Each user has use of the entire bandwidth during its assigned time slot.

terminal emulation A mechanism for users to interface over a network to applications running on a centralized computer. VT-220, 3270, and 5250 are types of terminal emulation.

transceiver A device that both transmits and receives information. The transceiver resides in a radio NIC.

VPN (virtual private network) The use of special software on the client device that controls access to remote applications and secures the connection from end to end using encryption.

WEP (Wired Equivalent Privacy) A part of the 802.11 standard that defines encryption between devices connected to a wireless LAN.

Wi-Fi A brand name given to wireless LANs that comply with standards as defined and published by the Wi-Fi Alliance. Wi-Fi standards are based on the 802.11 standard.

Wi-Fi Protected Access (WPA) A security protocol, defined by the Wi-Fi Alliance, that enables computer devices to periodically obtain a new encryption key. WPA version 1 implements Temporal Key Integrity Protocol (TKIP) and WEP; whereas, WPA version 2 implements the full 802.11i standard (which includes AES).

wireless LAN A network that satisfies wireless networking needs within the area of a building or college campus. 802.11 and Wi-Fi are popular standards defining wireless LANs.

wireless MAN A network that satisfies wireless networking needs within the area of a city. Wireless MANs make use of 802.16 and proprietary standards.

wireless PAN A network that satisfies wireless networking needs within a small room or reach of a person. Bluetooth and 802.15 are popular technologies for wireless PANs.

wireless WAN   A network that satisfies wireless networking needs over a large geographical area, such as a country or continent. Satellites offer a means for extending radio signals over a wireless WAN.

WISP (wireless Internet service provider)   A company that offers wireless connection services to the Internet for homes and offices. WISPs often provide wireless access in public wireless LAN hotspots.

INDEX

Q-R

DISCUSS
NETWORKING PRODUCTS AND TECHNOLOGIES WITH CISCO EXPERTS AND NETWORKING PROFESSIONALS WORLDWIDE

VISIT NETWORKING PROFESSIONALS
A CISCO ONLINE COMMUNITY
WWW.CISCO.COM/GO/DISCUSS

CISCO SYSTEMS

THIS IS THE POWER OF THE NETWORK. now.

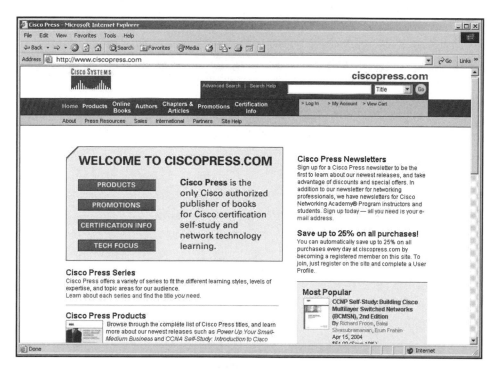

SEARCH THOUSANDS
OF BOOKS FROM
LEADING PUBLISHERS

Safari® Bookshelf is a searchable electronic reference library for IT professionals that features more than 2,000 titles from technical publishers, including Cisco Press.

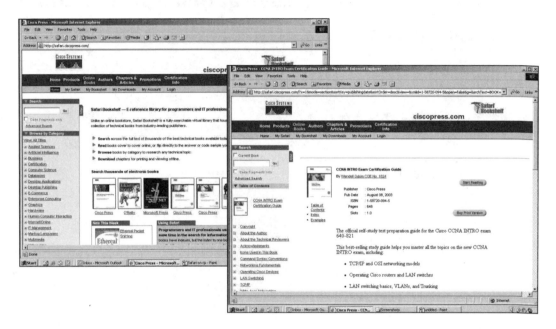

With Safari Bookshelf you can

- **Search** the full text of thousands of technical books, including more than 70 Cisco Press titles from authors such as Wendell Odom, Jeff Doyle, Bill Parkhurst, Sam Halabi, and Karl Solie.

- **Read** the books on My Bookshelf from cover to cover, or just flip to the information you need.

- **Browse** books by category to research any technical topic.

- **Download** chapters for printing and viewing offline.

With a customized library, you'll have access to your books when and where you need them—and all you need is a user name and password.

TRY SAFARI BOOKSHELF FREE FOR 14 DAYS!

You can sign up to get a 10-slot Bookshelf free for the first 14 days.
Visit **http://safari.ciscopress.com** to register.

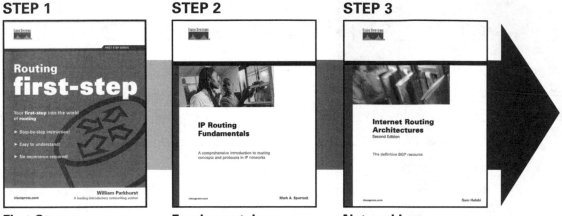